What Readers a

"I was a Nurse but . . . my Dad . . . wanted to die in his own home . . . . How quickly my sorrow gave way to peace when Dad looked in my eyes and said, 'Thank you,' before he slipped away. In this book, Anne gives all of us the knowledge to gain that same peace for our parents." —*Donna Martin, RN, home care supervisor.*

" . . . I wish I'd had Rachin's book when trying to navigate the ins and outs of home care for both my 90-year-old father and my paraplegic husband. —*Gail Mangurian, South Shore, Massachusetts.*

" . . . I thoroughly enjoyed her heartwarming stories which illustrate how home care services are vital for many seniors . . . and how these services can be tailored to meet the needs of the individual. I encourage anyone to read this book!" —*Kathy Spameni, primary caregiver.*

"Rachin tackles the sensitive subject of caring for the elderly with a professional, yet compassionate voice. This book opened my eyes to the fact that living out the last years of one's life with dignity is best done in one's own home. Period." —*Jen Forcino, critic for the paper "Brooklynville" Brooklyn, NY.*

"This book [is] a hopeful vision for us all as we begin to consider how to manage the best interests of our aging loved ones . . . . 'Aging In Place' offers an option that reclaims dignity and real personal choice for seniors and their families." —*Nicole Conneally, Chepachet, RI.*

ALL THAT'S FAMILIAR
Anne R. Rachin

Also available in Kindle, Nook and ePub formats
Manufactured in the United States of America

ISBN: 978-1-937327-15-6
Library of Congress Control Number: 2012952883
Copyright © 2012 by Anne R. Rachin

Moonshine Cove Publishing, LLC
150 Willow Pt
Abbeville, SC 29620.

Books that Beckon

Book design by Moonshine Cove; cover image from author.

*For my Dad, who made it possible
to do what I love,
and to my staff and caregivers who
make it possible to love what I do.*

All the Best,
Anne R. Rockin

Table of Contents

Acknowledgments

This project began with my hope and a folder marked 'BOOK SOMEDAY'. The faith that I could actually do it came from Mary Jane Smith, a loyal employee and cherished friend. Her belief in the project filled the folder over the years and provided the motivation for me to begin the actual writing six years ago. I am grateful to Mary Jane for taking her personal time to read the initial very rough draft with critical eye and giving me the feedback that set the tone for revisions and ultimately the final draft. Mary Jane has dedicated her career to home care and has never wavered from that commitment to keeping individuals at home to end of life.

My thanks goes to my oldest of friends, Jane Moore, who unknowingly, during her periods of crisis with aging parents, reinforced my determination to complete this much-needed home care resource guide.

Deepest appreciation to my parents and brother who believed in my dream three decades ago and provided continuous support over the years. My Dad died in 2002 at home. My Mom is an inspiration to this day. Nearly 90 years old, she lives independently in her own home.

To my publisher and editor, Gene Robinson, of Moonshine Cove Publishing, thank you for taking a risk on a novice author, realizing the importance of my message and working fervently with me by e-mail and phone to produce a book of which we both can be proud.

And last, but my no means least, I give a heartfelt thank you to my husband, Barry, and to my daughters Lana and Hannah. Thank you Barry for taking on the difficult task of editing my book - rough and revised drafts - page by page, with me looking over your shoulder, and managing the impossible – the perfect balance between 'ding' and 'quibble'. Adults have the maturity to understand when time constraints don't allow for chores to get done – why the house is messy, the laundry unfolded, or the dishes piled high in the sink. Children do not! I am blessed with two daughters who are both patient and kind to a mother who constantly lost track of time these past six years. I seriously began the writing of this book, pencil to paper, while they took skating lessons eight o'clock on Saturday mornings, and oftentimes missed their hard-earned jumps or perfect spirals. They rarely complained. There were exasperated sighs when, once again, they were the last waiting at school to be picked up; looks of frustration when I pleaded for yet another ten minutes to type a revision; disbelief when I forgot our beloved dog, Theodore, outside in the back yard and he wandered off, eventually ending up at the pound. Thank you, Lana and Hannah for understanding more than complaining, for believing in me – I love you!

"What we do for ourselves dies with us. What we do for others and the world remains and is immortal"

—Albert Pine

INTRODUCTION

Scanning the room, my eyes always stopped at the photographs. Curiosity invariably prompted me to ask about a particular picture. This was part of the process of becoming familiar with each new client. Initially, I thought the young face behind the frame was a son or daughter. It took a while for me, in the early days of my career, to grasp that the voluptuous girl posing on the hood of the vintage car or the muscular young man gripping the tennis racket, was in fact the same person sitting before me, now aged and frail.

The majority of individuals that I have provided home care service for over these past thirty years have been frail elderly. Yet they were all young once! And each comes with a story.

Some, like Pearl and Thelma were pioneers. Pearl was the first female in her family and community to drive a car —on the freeway too! Thelma broke through the 'glass ceiling' before women knew there was one. Never married, she chose to be a career woman, becoming the senior buyer for a large city department store. Her job required frequent trips to Europe for new merchandise. Whenever Thelma talked about Christmas time at the store you could picture yourself as a child again, waiting in line to see Santa Claus.

The stories of love touch deeply. For Henry, it was mustering enough nerve to ask his best friend's sister to the senior prom. They eventually married and raised five children together.

Some are of sadness—the young immigrant couple whose first-borne child succumbed to influenza during the 1918 pandemic. Another was the 1940s teenage mother who never saw her baby because 'good' girls refrained from pre-marital sex.

Carmella was married for forty-seven years, raising two sons, both successful businessmen. Now at 94, she lives alone in a one bedroom apartment. This soft-spoken, silver-haired woman reminisces about herself as a single, 19-year-old working her first job in a downtown office. A co-worker, a couple of years older, invited her out after work to celebrate her birthday. She did not dare tell her parents but instead feigned having to work late to meet a project deadline. The dinner went perfectly, until the check came and her co-worker realized his wallet was left at home. Her pale blue eyes brighten and her thin weathered lips part in a smile as she recounts having to pay for her own birthday celebration. He was her first love! Then her smile fades, her voice becomes a whisper. He went off to war and never made it back.

Frances, a gifted pianist, had her dreams of studying at Julliard obliterated when she contracted polio. Left with debilitating pain and disfiguring mobility, she kept the music alive by teaching piano to neighborhood children. Her health continued to decline as she aged, and she suffered hearing loss as well. However, when this amazing woman sat down in front of the piano, her fingers moved like those of a young girl and her music—whether it be a lyrical rendition of Beethoven's *Moonlight Sonata* or a funky Scott Joplin ragtime—resonated throughout the room.

The chapters of their life are unique to each, but the final chapter for all reads the same—they wanted to remain at home until end of life. I have committed my career to making this possible.

A home care administrator since 1982, I own and operate Ideal Home Care Service in North Providence, Rhode Island along with my husband, Barry. We employ homemakers and certified nursing assistants (aides) and match them with clients who wish to remain living in their own home, rather than nursing homes or similar facilities. Our services enable individuals to live at home independently, all for a fraction of what it would cost in an institution. Although home care service is provided to young as well as old, the focus of this book is seniors who want to age in place.

Seniors are the fastest growing group in this country. Close to 90% want to stay put in their home as well as the community that they have been a part of for many years. Yet most individuals do not give much thought to aging in place or long term care until they are faced with a medical crisis. A recent AARP survey indicates that 64% of adults require assistance with daily living tasks such as laundry, meal preparation, grocery shopping, housework and personal care. These individuals want to remain at home! They want to avoid both the physical and emotional trauma of leaving all that is familiar and moving to an institutional facility where they are compelled to live alongside people with no shared history! But oftentimes, this is exactly what happens. As well as being more cost effective, home care is a viable option in most cases, but individuals are often unaware of this choice. They are not cognizant that home care exists because it is seldom promoted. In today's economy, it makes infinite sense for state officials to implement home care programs, rather than diminish budgets paying for institutionalized care. Nursing home care in this country can range from $200 to $500 per day whereas home care costs considerably less. Over the past thirty years, I have witnessed numerous instances of families in crisis making long-term care decisions under pressure and without full knowledge of their options. Too often I hear families say, after the fact, that, if they had only known about home care, they would never have placed their mother, father or other loved one in an institution. Placement oftentimes results in feelings of guilt and letting a loved one down.

I have received calls at home from personal friends faced with an aging parent in crisis and not knowing where to begin. The genesis of this book emerged from my realization that the elder care system in our country neither favors nor supports keeping an individual at home. The following chapters will provide the reader with various examples of how home care service can assist an individual to age in place. I also look ahead to the next generation, the baby boomers, and how I believe this unique group will handle growing old in America.

This book is about making the choice to remain living at home and should be used as a do-it-yourself, resource guide to achieve that goal. Meant to assist individuals and families who wish to pursue home care, it does not judge other forms of care because not everyone can be maintained at home.

Also, personal situations and human conditions can change so that a relatively self-sufficient senior citizen living at home may not be able to remain there until death.

As I began my outline for this book I thought of the *Starfish Parable.* Thousands of starfish wash upon a beach and are slowly dying on the sun-baked sand. A man walking along the beach begins picking them up and tossing them back into the ocean. Another man comes along and comments that there are far too many starfish on the beach to save and that tossing any back will not make a difference. The first man picks up another starfish, tosses it into the ocean, and says "I made a difference to that one."

It is my intent in this book to share what I have learned about home care over the years and, if I can make a difference in one person's life, then I have been successful. It is my hope that the reader will be inspired to research, endorse and choose home care over institutional living.

To the unlearned, old age is winter time;
to the wise, old age is harvest time.
—Hasidic proverb

CHAPTER ONE
No Expiration Date

Grandma Moses worked as a farmer until late into her 70s. For relaxation she enjoyed embroidering. When she was 78 her fingers became too stiff for her to handle the needle, so she began to oil paint, and continued to do so right up to the time of her death at age 101. Frank Lloyd Wright designed the Guggenheim Museum at age 76. Albert Schweitzer won the Nobel Prize at age 68 and was still treating patients until he died at age 90. There is a group of senior citizens from North Hampton, MA who sing rock songs about the taboos of old age. They call themselves *Young At Heart* and perform worldwide. At age 93, Harry Bernstein wrote *The Invisible Wall,* a memoir of his early years in England; when he was 98 his second memoir, *The Dream*, was published. The list could go on for an entire chapter of seniors who continue to *'grow'* and contribute well beyond the age of retirement.

There is no denying that, as we age, our bodies go through physical, mental and emotional changes. However, growing old in this country should not mean the end of one's productivity or usefulness to society. Neither should it be a threat of having to leave one's home and community and be placed in a nursing home or other form of institutional living. Entry into a long term care facility insidiously strips away one's privileges, rights, and choices. Alice Brown, a 19th century writer, describes so poignantly in one of her short stories, the resignation of sequestered old ladies. These women, residents of an Old Ladies home set back from the road realize that active life was presumably over for them, and "all the more did they long to see the passing of the little world which had usurped their places." In the same vein, Tom Koch states in his 1993 book, *A Place In Time-Care Givers For Their Elderly,* "to be in an institution is to be outside the reach of one's community of history and to have finally relinquished the personal choices that, for most of us, are a large part of what makes us human beings."

By the year 2040, twenty percent of our country's population will be senior citizens. We cannot remain in denial. As more and more of our population live well into their 80s, 90s and even 100+, we need to revolutionize the way we care for our elders! The days of stay-at-home moms who assume the role of caregiver for aging parents is past, and multi-generational living under one roof today exists more for economics rather than age-related considerations.

Americans must become better educated about our aging society, including what medical concerns the aging process involves as well as the need for specialized geriatric care. One should focus on assessing immediate needs and formulating individualized long term care plans with emphasis on home based services. End of life directives must also be addressed. Given the choice, most elderly want to remain in their own home and die there. They should not be warehoused in old age institutions but rather remain in the community where they can interact with the outside world.

In most cases, home care is not only a viable option, but also is more cost effective. A homemaker assists with daily living tasks such as housework, laundry, meal preparation, grocery shopping and necessary errands. An aide can assist with personal care. In addition, *both* can provide emotional support, observe changes in client condition or family relationships and report these changes to their immediate supervisor who is responsible for the client care plan.

In my years of experience in the profession, I have seen where home care is not readily promoted as an option as much as it could be. Family members are often advised to apply for long term care placement for Mom or Dad well before there is a need, so that a bed is reserved in a facility "just in case." When an individual or family is in crisis, they can quickly become panicked or overwhelmed and make a hasty decision. Many individuals are not aware that they have the option to return home after a hospital discharge because the dynamics of home care are not fully explained nor understood. The following chapters give examples of how home care services can be put in place and assist an individual or family to remain living independently in their own home.

UNIVERSITY OF RHODE ISLAND: COLLEGE
OF CONTINUING EDUCATION
COURSE AND SECTION: AGN004
HOME CARE FOR THE ELDERLY: A
PRACTICAL APPROACH TO
INDEPENDENT LIVING
WEDNESDAY: 7:00 PM

CHAPTER TWO
Cancelled for lack of interest

In the Fall of 1982 I was scheduled to teach a course on Home Care at the URI Campus of Continuing Education. I was enthusiastic about the opportunity to share what I knew about aging in place and my belief that everyone should have the option to remain living at home until death. I knew then, nearly thirty years ago, that home care was enabling individuals to live independently with minimal assistance and at a fraction of the cost of institutionalized care. Unfortunately, not everyone shared my enthusiasm or conviction nor did they have the desire to learn about this practical approach to independent living. The course was *cancelled* due to insufficient enrollment!

Home care is not new. As early as 1780, Boston City Hospital offered a home care program staffed by social workers and paramedical personnel. Referrals came from inpatient and out-patient services, as well as community referrals.

In the 19th century the sick were primarily cared for at

home. Usually the caregiver was the mother, or eldest female in the family. Social and sometimes financial support was given by extended family, friends and neighbors. Only those without family or support of any kind were confined to a hospital or asylum. By the end of the century, however, many of the wealthy and upper class came to view home care as an interference with their social life. The field of medicine was advancing, and along with these advancements came the construction of institutions to care for the homebound.

The twentieth century became known as the hospital or institution-oriented society. The Social Security Act of 1935 was intended by Congress to provide income security for growing numbers of seniors. However, Congress would not disburse assistance funds to individuals in public institutions, because they wanted to encourage elderly to live at home or with foster families. This resulted in a mass exodus from public institutions to privately owned, for-profit boarding homes. Over time, these boarding homes began to add nurses and became known as *nursing homes.* By the mid-1950s substantial growth had taken place in the nursing home industry. But the greatest boom was yet to come with the enactment of Medicare & Medicaid in 1965. Nursing homes changed from a family enterprise to big business, with large corporations, including motels and hotels becoming major purchasers. More than 75% of nursing homes were owned by for profit interests at this time, with the primary contractor for these services being the Federal Government.

As nursing home populations grew nationwide, so did problems. Complaints of over-medicating, poor nutrition, harsh physical handling of patients, and inadequate care caused major concern in Washington, DC. The 1970s called for stricter regulations in nursing home operations along with a cry to end government reimbursement for substandard facilities.

By the time Ideal Home Care opened its doors in 1982, we had been through a great deal of changes in this country, from war abroad to protest movements at home. We had seen four students shot dead by National Guardsman at Kent State University; President Nixon resign rather than be impeached; and the worst recession in forty years. This new decade became known as the "me" years. Adrienne Rich's poem, "In Those Years, "captures the 1980s best by describing that period as a time when self-absorbed individuals lost track of the communal sense and thus: " . . . we found ourselves reduced to I . . . ."

A new type of billionaire emerged as a result of buyouts, takeovers and mergers. Splurging and buying on credit became the norm, with the slogan "shop 'til you drop."

The women's movement in this country inspired females to take jobs outside the home. Having previously been the primary caregivers to their aged loved ones, this left a growing   elderly population to fend for themselves. Determined to remain independent, yet needing some assistance with daily living tasks, home care services began to fill these needs. Initially, our home care employees were identified as Homemakers, but as the industry became more regulated, their role became more restrictive. Once able to help a client with personal care, a Homemaker can now assist with household tasks only. A trained and certified Aide provides hands-on personal care.

The 1990s became a decade of world-wide changes. Communist rule ended in the Soviet Union, East and West Germany became a unified country again, Nelson Mandela was released from prison after twenty-seven years, and the world wide web was created. Advanced medical technology resulted in Americans living longer. With the graying of America, came the awareness that we, as a society, needed to change the way we treat our elderly.

In 2006, Val J. Halamandaris, editor and publisher of *Caring*, noted that the government expended approximately $7,000 whenever a Medicare patient was admitted through a hospital emergency room. Once these patients enter a nursing home and are no longer able to pay, Medicaid, the health care program for indigents, picks up the tab, further bankrupting resources. With our country now suffering deficits in the trillions, these health care services are prohibitive (i.e. no longer affordable). Keeping an individual at home makes economic sense and we should be promoting a service that *saves* every tax payer money without impoverishing future generations. The facts can no longer be ignored. As individuals continue to live longer, issues of long term care must be addressed. To this end, home care offers the optimal benefit—maintaining patient dignity while keeping costs affordable.

"Life comes down to a series of choices.
The only choice not available to me is
whether or not I have Parkinson's.
The rest is up for grabs."
—Michael J. Fox

CHAPTER THREE
Parkinson's: Not Part Of The Plan

The first symptoms Bill C. felt were tremors in his hands and loss of balance. Odd jobs that he loved to do around the house became dreaded chores. Bill eventually began having trouble sleeping, difficulty swallowing which caused choking spells, and emotional upsets—all symptoms of Parkinson's Disease (PD). After learning that he had PD, Bill went through a period of severe depression, which is common, but with medical treatment as well as ongoing support and encouragement from his wife, Lucy, Bill came to accept the disease and modified his life accordingly.

Bill and Lucy met at a wedding in June, 1943. He knew the groom. She was best friends with the bride's sister. Because the country was at war and Bill expected to ship out to Europe after boot camp, they married following a brief courtship. Returning home after the war, Bill decided to use his GI bill for schooling. Lucy worked in a fabric mill until becoming pregnant with their son. In early 1950, the young family bought a home in the suburbs. Bill got a job as a high school science teacher and Lucy became a stay-at-home mom.

The years passed quickly. Their only son, Ted, married and soon Bill and Lucy became grandparents. In his early 60s, Bill retired from teaching. His plan was to travel with Lucy, enjoy the role of doting grandfather and to grow old gracefully. Parkinson's was not part of the plan! Nor was Lucy's untimely death.

Bill's daughter-in-law, Gwen, contacted our agency shortly after Lucy died. Hearing about us from a member in her father-in-law's Parkinson support group, she wanted Bill to have a home care assessment. Bill was 71 years old, no longer driving, and adamant about remaining in his home without outside help.

Our geriatric care specialist met with Bill. Understandably, he was still mourning Lucy's death. Bill felt that, being the needier of the two, Lucy should not have died first. Not only was Bill resentful about losing his life partner of fifty-two years, but also feared facing an uncertain future alone.

We explained to Bill that the purpose of home care was to provide assistance with daily living tasks, enabling individuals like him to remain living independently while also affording respite for family. Bill received excellent support from Ted and Gwen. They took him grocery shopping every Saturday and prepared his meals. However, having their own family responsibilities precluded them from doing more. Because Bill's laundry room was in the basement, Ted feared that his father would fall trying to negotiate the stairs while carrying a basket of clothes. In addition, Ted and Gwen worried that Bill would become isolated. Bill resisted the notion of receiving help from anyone, stating he could do his own housework and that his washing machine and dryer did the laundry! In truth, Bill was holding onto his grief. After calming down, he confided how difficult it was to accept Parkinson's and its limitations. While she was alive, Lucy's unwavering support bolstered his resolve.

As he shared memories, Bill became increasingly emotional. Pointing to a photo collage on the wall that Ted and Gwen put together for Bill and Lucy's thirty-fifth wedding anniversary, Bill excitedly provided details of each picture. The glass-domed mantel clock with rotating pendulum chimed the hour and triggered another memory for Bill—watching the evening news with Lucy. They knew when to put the TV on by the sounding of the chimes. Looking out into the backyard at a scattering of earth-colored autumn leaves, Bill *sees* his son as a young boy jumping into a newly raked pile of leaves. Bill's memories extend back more than forty years in this home and community. This is where he wants to stay! Bill came to the realization that he *could* remain here, where all is familiar, but needed help to do so.

We matched Bill with Dee, an aide experienced with clients suffering a chronic progressive disease. Dee was scheduled two hours per day, twice a week. Tuesday was designated laundry day. On Thursday, Dee vacuumed, dusted, cleaned the bathroom and kitchen and washed the floors. When leaving, Dee also took Bill's garbage to the trash barrel. Bill adapted to the new routine quickly. Looking forward to Dee's twice-weekly scheduled visits, Bill relished talking about what he did with his grandchildren or shared what he learned at his support group meeting. Bill was relieved that he no longer felt compelled to do housework and laundry, even admitting that he got tired just watching Dee at work.

Although Bill's Parkinson's did not progress rapidly, his family was aware that, as he continued to age, this chronic, debilitating disease would worsen, requiring Bill to need more care at home. A home care plan can be modified as often as necessary to meet a client's changing circumstances. Should Bill need assistance with personal care, an aide would be assigned. If Bill wanted Dee to continue as his homemaker, personal care would be added on different days. When personal care is required daily, this component is generally scheduled in the morning hours and housework later in the day. We avoid scheduling two caregivers at the same time. A care plan is left in the client's home by our agency nurse and specifies which tasks each home care employee performs.

Bill's son and daughter-in-law soon found that having extra support generated free time each week for their own family needs. At one point, they requested a temporary increase in Bill's service, to allow them a much needed vacation together.

To date, there is no cure for Parkinson's Disease. More than half a million people in the United States suffer from this neurological disorder, among them former champion boxer, Mohammed Ali, and famous actor, Michael J. Fox. This number will only increase as more people live longer. A viable, first-choice option, home care allows compromised individuals to remain safely at home, while providing peace of mind to concerned love ones.

*"The happiness of most people is not
ruined by great catastrophes or fatal
errors, but by the repetition of slowly
destructive little things."*

— Ernest Dimnet

CHAPTER FOUR
Slow Destruction

The ever-growing problem of obesity in this country has caused an increase of Type 2 Diabetes in both adults and children. In recent years, our agency has recognized an increased need for home care service to diabetic clients. Insulin in our body regulates the blood sugars or glucose, which we need for energy. When the body is unable to use insulin properly, glucose does not enter the cells, precipitating a build-up in the blood stream with resulting high blood sugar levels. Over time this extra sugar can damage heart, nerves, blood vessels, kidneys and eyes. It is very important for individuals to maintain good eating habits, stay physically active and know if there is a family history of diabetes.

Len S. began home care service with us upon hospital discharge. He had been rushed to the emergency room after suffering an eye hemorrhage, caused by his diabetic condition, which resulted in the loss of vision in one eye. Because Len's wife, Edith, did not drive, they needed homemaker service for grocery shopping and necessary errands. Len also required assistance with diabetic meal preps as well as motivation to begin a daily exercise routine.

Len was a retired postal worker. He began his career as a slim, energetic rookie walking his first mail delivery route. In time, Len was promoted to a managerial position, putting him behind a desk all day. He began gaining weight, which prompted another bad habit—cigar smoking. Developing high blood pressure, his doctor prescribed medication to manage the hypertensive condition and cautioned him about a sedentary lifestyle and the risk of type 2 diabetes. But Len continued his destructive behavior pattern. By the time he retired at age 65, the former postal worker was overweight, a self-described couch potato, and suffering from chronic high blood pressure along with diabetes.

After retiring, Len continued to neglect his health. He failed to eat a balanced diet, or monitor his blood sugars on a daily basis. Most days, especially during winter months, Len never exercised. He was at high risk for diabetic retinopathy, which is damage to the eye's retina caused by long-term diabetes.

Len's crisis struck early one morning as he sat down to read the newspaper. His vision was blurry and he could not focus. He then began to experience pain. He said, " It was like a shade falling in front of my eyes—everything turned to dark." At the emergency room, Len admitted to the triage nurse that he had been experiencing intermittent vision problems the last few weeks. The result of Len's negligence was the loss of vision in one eye and legal blindness in the other. This proved to be a major life-changing crisis for him.

His first concern was for his wife, Edith, who routinely depended on him to drive her wherever she needed to go. Len and Edith had a son who lived in Chicago. Unable to travel the long distance to assist his parents, instead he located our agency on the internet and contracted for home care services. It was a great relief to know that home care assistance would be in place upon his father's hospital discharge. Today, many families are separated by miles and rely on cyberspace to locate and contract for services long distance.

We matched Len with Olga, one of our aides. Having diabetic parents, Olga was very knowledgeable about the disease. She understood how difficult it was for Len to adjust to vision loss, not to mention surrendering his driver's license. Not wanting to lose more of his independence and fiercely determined to remain living in his community, Len was amenable to outside help.

Olga quickly familiarized herself with Edith's shopping routine, which afforded Len tremendous relief. Len's care plan included meal preparation with an emphasis on proper diet while encouraging exercise. Olga educated him about how foods he ate affected his blood sugars. Soon, she also began walking with Len around the block every day. To keep him motivated, Edith joined them, and in relatively short time all three began longer walks to a nearby park. Len started to lose weight and feel more energetic. It was a bit more difficult for Olga to alter Len's nightly routine of enjoying a cigar after supper. But over time, she was successful. Len's crisis with diabetes was warning enough for him to pay strict attention and make the necessary health changes. He and Edith were able to remain in their own home and neighborhood. And although Len could no longer drive, they remained active in the community by utilizing their local senior van services.

It has been almost two years since Len started receiving home care service from our agency. He has successfully monitored his diabetes, without a single additional emergency room visit. Olga still does the weekly grocery shopping, walks with Len to the nearby park and has seen a dramatic improvement in his quality of life.

We are each of us angels
with only one wing
and we can only fly
by embracing one another
— Luciano de Crescenzo

CHAPTER FIVE
Unsung Heroes

They work days, evenings, weekends—sometimes seven days a week. Snow doesn't keep them home, nor does a summer heat wave. And to take Thanksgiving Day and Christmas Day off in-house staff must assure them that meals will be delivered to a needy client. They become like family to those who have none. "They" are the dedicated caregivers who provide assistance with daily living tasks enabling an individual to remain at home. At Ideal Home Care our titles are homemaker and aide. Elsewhere they may be known as personal care assistant, cna, or home health aide. The title may vary, but their role is similar. When the right match is made, this team of caregiver and client can be together for many years.

Their job with our agency begins with an application and interview process. An aide in Rhode Island must carry an active license from the Department of Health, with renewal every two years. All applicants are thoroughly screened using previous employers, personal references and criminal investigation check before they are hired. Once accepted, a new employee receives orientation prior to assignment. Going forward, we continue to monitor work performance, ensuring that a good match has been made between caregiver and client.

An aide from Ideal Home Care Service is responsible for personal care tasks, such as bathing, shampooing, shaving and helping a client dress. They also perform light housework, vacuum, change bed linens, laundry, meal preparation, grocery shopping and necessary errands.

A homemaker can perform the same tasks as an aide with the notable exception of personal care.

Rather than utilize a per-diem system, Ideal Home Care always matches a client with a specific caregiver. We do this for the following reasons:

— to establish a long-term relationship between client and caregiver
— to avoid frequent change, which can confuse and overwhelm a client
— to provide respite and support for spouse and/or other family members
— to ensure consistency, which allows the caregiver to immediately spot a change in client condition and report it to their supervisor. This greatly helps home care achieve its primary goal, to assist individuals in continuing to live independently.

Understandably, an individual may feel hesitant allowing a stranger into their home for assistance to remain living independently. A client or family member may feel more secure directly hiring someone (gray market) rather than trusting the process to an agency. Costs can be lower going it alone. However, the risks can far outweigh the benefits. With an established licensed agency clients secure the services of a pre-screened, trained and supervised employee. Additionally, an agency carries the necessary workman's compensation, liability and bonding insurance, that a client who is acting as employer, would otherwise be responsible for. Clients also benefit from knowing that an agency representative is available to respond to any questions or concerns. Significantly, agencies are mandated to adhere to HIPPA (Health Insurance Portability and Accountability Act) which protects individuals' medical privacy, requiring all employees to maintain strict confidentiality.

To be kind is to truly care about the needs of another individual. Simply stated, *kindness* is the one quality that homemakers and aides have in common. They share tears with a client whose cancer has returned, or is grieving the loss of a loved one. There can be the knock on the door that goes unanswered by a client. Caregivers sometimes have had to secure the assistance of the local authorities to gain access to a client's home and have found them deceased—a painfully difficult way to say good-bye.

I recall an aide coming into my office sobbing on a Monday morning after learning that one of her clients died in her sleep the previous night, and another had been hospitalized over the weekend. Another case involved a terminally ill client receiving daily service. Initially, the aide requested weekends off, but after bonding with this client, stated that she could not leave her from Friday to Monday knowing that the end was so near. She wanted to be there to comfort and fulfill a final wish to die at home, surrounded by familiar sights, sounds and smells.

This is kindness. It begins on the first day of service, when an anxious client opens the door and is greeted by a caregiver who quickly puts them at ease. This skilled individual will introduce herself. She will learn such things as a client's dietary likes and dislikes, how often the bed linen needs changing, shopping day, and any physical limitations. They will not judge a client by the amount of clutter or the cleanliness of their home. Genuine kindness is the only way to characterize the caregiver who always has something nice to say about the client who finds fault with everything. Most would label such an individual a chronic complainer, but a caregiver who is genuinely kind will say things such as, "they are in pain, or they are not feeling well or they are having a difficult time with the aging process." And who, but someone with this unique quality can shower and dress an individual, only to have them soil themselves, and cleanse them all over again without stripping that person of their dignity? Only someone truly kind, refrains from telling a person with dementia that they have heard "their story" so many times that they can repeat it verbatim. No, instead they listen patiently and respond with amazement at the story's ending.

With all the responsibilities and hard work that operating a home care agency entails, my job is negligible to that of homemakers and aides.

If wrinkles must be written upon our brow,
let them not be written upon the heart,
the spirit should not grow old.
                                    —James A. Garfield

CHAPTER SIX
Red Is For The Heart

Lisa knows that heart disease is the #1 killer of women and men in America. Post-menopausal women are at higher risk to suffer heart attacks. Because warning signs for women are different than men, many women who suffer a heart attack are not even aware until it is too late. Lisa is familiar with these facts because her company participates in the annual *Red for Women* campaign. Each year on the first Friday in February, Lisa wears red to work and takes part in this healthy heart awareness promotion.

Sophia, an active octogenarian, still grew her own vegetables and preserved her harvest every fall. She walked each day to church for morning services. If she wanted a newspaper, she strolled an extra two blocks to the neighborhood convenience store. Oftentimes, when stopping by to visit, Lisa found her mother making a pizza or putting finishing touches on a freshly baked dessert.

Then the day came when Lisa dropped in to see her mother during lunch break, and immediately knew the older woman was experiencing a heart attack. It did not take much for Lisa to notice that her mother was not well, because she was dozing on her recliner with a cold cup of tea on a side tray. Sophia explained to Lisa that she had gone out earlier that morning and on her walk home, experienced a tightness in her chest and shortness of breath. She also was nauseous and felt lightheaded. As is frequently the case with most heart attack victims, Sophia came home, took a Tylenol, and rested. She felt that it was probably indigestion and would soon pass.

Lisa immediately took her mother to the hospital emergency room. Blood work and an EKG confirmed that Sophia had suffered a heart attack. Following a stent placement, Sophia was released home from the hospital with anti-clotting and cholesterol-lowering medications. If it can be performed soon after the heart attack, angioplasty with stent placement is the treatment of choice. The procedure opens a narrowed artery, thus increasing blood flow to the heart. Angioplasty is less invasive than by-pass surgery and recovery time is quicker.

Heart attack victims oftentimes are hesitant about resuming a manageable schedule and for this reason run the risk of becoming sedentary. Sophia's doctor recommended that, upon hospital discharge, she return to a modified daily routine. While at the hospital visiting her mother, Lisa picked up one of our agency brochures. She knew Sophia would resist personal care, but agreed to some short-term help with household tasks such as vacuuming, changing the bed linens and laundry.

During our initial assessment it became clear that both Lisa and Sophia were concerned about nutrition. Lisa wanted her mother to eat healthy and Sophia wanted to make changes to her diet that would promote getting better and staying that way. Setting up the service, we chose Maria, a homemaker who coincidentally was an excellent cook. Recognizing that food was an essential part of Sophia's identity, the emphasis in this instance was on the preparation of healthy meals rather than the actual cooking. Maria warned Sophia about high cholesterol foods and rich desserts, explaining how she could utilize low-fat substitutes such as ripened fruit, when baking. She also cautioned her about processed, white flour and oil-soaked pizzas. Sophia reluctantly agreed to switch to a salt substitute, a difficult change to make since she admitted to being a heavy salt user most of her life. Before her heart attack, Sophia loved Chinese food, but after reviewing the nutritional literature received at the hospital, realized that she could only indulge this passion on rare occasions.

Sophia's service plan included light housework, vacuuming and assistance with laundry. Maria supported Sophia's desire to resume an active lifestyle by granting her every opportunity to assist with domestic tasks. For example, Maria carried the laundry basket up and down the stairs for Sophia, but readily allowed the older woman to wash, fold and put her clothes away.

Because Sophia was highly motivated to get well and return to an active routine, she followed Maria's advice on meal preparations and accepted her help with the household tasks. In no time at all, Sophia resumed daily walks and her gardening. As our homemaker service came to an end, Sophia was busy perusing seed catalogs and anxiously awaiting Spring.

National Wear Red Day is observed on the first Friday in February. The campaign was started in 2002 by the American Heart Association to raise awareness about the seriousness of heart disease in women. Americans nationwide wear red on this day in support of women's heart disease awareness.

Memories
You have sweet memories of what we did and said all
clear and vivid runnin' through your head
Every single Christmas, Santa all in red
Even little secrets from out behind the shed
We could sit and laugh and talk away the hours
'Bout little spotted frogs and nice warm thundershowers
Then the years flew past me and age had lined my face
And even when I read I would often lose my place
Now here in the evening of my life far away from dawn
You are grieving for my memories that you think are gone
But I have every single one oh right from the very start For
when they left my head I tucked them safely in my heart.
—Ken Freeman

CHAPTER SEVEN
Keeper of My Memories

When in college studying gerontology, I read a book about dementia, written by the main character's grandson. He tells the story of his grandfather's decline, which began with forgetting things such as where his car keys were, and getting lost while driving home. The book details his deterioration leading to death. It was a graphic account about the grandfather choosing to end his life by ceasing all forms of nourishment. He made this final choice while still cognizant because he did not want to become a burden to anyone, or worse yet, be institutionalized. It was not until years later that I realized this man probably suffered Alzheimer's disease.

In 1984 Ideal Home Care began providing care for Alzheimer patients at home. At that time, there were no community programs, and very little was known about this degenerative disease. Alzheimer's could only be diagnosed post-mortem after an autopsy was done of the brain. A key resource for us was a book entitled *The Thirty-Six Hour Day*, published by Johns Hopkins University. This insidious disease, precipitated by memory loss, still has no cure. Although age is a high risk factor, research has shown that good nutrition, regular exercise, and remaining involved in one's community may slow down the disease's progression.

Margaret's daughter was quick to explain that the person she was about to introduce me to was not the same person who had brought her up and planned her fairy-book wedding. Nor was she the same woman who loved sleepovers with her grandchildren and spoiling them with shopping trips to the local mall. This woman, now in her mid-70s, was quickly becoming a stranger to all who loved her. She could be kind and mellow one moment, rude and combative the next. Some days she greeted her grandchildren by name but only moments later responded to them as though they were strangers. Also, her once impeccable appearance became slovenly. Some mornings she stubbornly refused to get out of bed. Other days, she got up but clearly hadn't bathed or changed her rumpled clothes. When I asked about meal preparation, Margaret's daughter was embarrassed to say that her mother had to be closely monitored when eating because the prior weekend, at a family gathering, she gorged on watermelon to the point of eating seeds and all. This disease was taking its toll on all family members involved, and had institutional care been an option in the mid-1980s, we may never have been contacted. But Alzheimer's was still a medical mystery, and there were no nursing homes in the nearby suburban community accepting patients with this disease. Today, there are separate facilities dedicated solely to the care of the victims of Alzheimer's Disease.

Our initial assessment resulted in setting up a caregiver for Margaret three days per week. This also gave her daughter, with whom she lived, some respite time. We matched Margaret with Carol, a middle-aged compassionate woman with a smile that lit up the room when she walked in. Carol decided to become a caregiver after nursing both her parents at end of their life. She was a patient and self-assured individual, and did not personalize any negative behavior that Margaret displayed or verbalized. Oftentimes a person with Alzheimer's will respond inappropriately because they become confused, disoriented, even frightened. They may be searching for something, a wallet, magazine or pair of glasses, but cannot remember what, or may have forgotten how to do basic tasks such as brew a cup of tea. An experienced caregiver knows to calmly show their client where the "misplaced" item is, or explain in a patient manner how to place the tea bag into a cup and enjoy the tea. Some Alzheimer clients experience catastrophic reactions. For example, they may become extremely combative when the tub or shower is turned on for bathing. Others have *sundowning* or roaming episodes. Sundowning occurs at night, with the client becoming agitated and restless because they have "forgotten" why it gets dark and what the purpose of this time is for—i.e. sleeping. They may roam about the house, or run the risk of walking away from home and becoming lost.

Carol attended workshops we offered at Ideal, learning all she could about the Alzheimer patient. She assisted Margaret with dressing, meals and reality testing during the two hours of service. Reality testing consisted of Carol greeting and saying her name to Margaret. She then mentioned what day of the week it was, and a current event, attempting to engage Margaret in conversation. We also installed a wipe-off board in the kitchen. Carol used this for day of the week, season of the year, and upcoming events such as a birthday or a grandchild's school play. Carol learned about catastrophic reactions that occur with Alzheimer patients causing them to become frightened by such things as running water, which was why Margaret no longer bathed on a regular basis. To prevent Margaret from wandering, we asked the family to install a slip latch higher up on the door, knowing that she would never remember to look up to unlock it. The routine and consistency helped Margaret stay at home, and home care provided a much-needed respite for her daughter.

Today, our agency continues to service Alzheimer patients, keeping them safely at home. Many of them attend adult day care, which is geared specifically to individuals with Alzheimer's. We provide early morning personal care service for these clients, helping them bathe and dress before putting them on the day care shuttle. Oftentimes, our aide returns to take them off the bus at end of day, prepare a meal, and ready them for bed. Home care service gives needed respite to an overwhelmed spouse or other family, and keeps a loved one at home for as long as possible.

Author's Note:

In 2010, Brad Pitman of Attleboro, MA published a memoir, entitled Ma Is Back, about his mother, who had been diagnosed with Alzheimer's Disease. The book documents how his mother's memory was restored with certain foods and supplements. His discovery began when he gave her an ear of yellow corn to eat and she devoured it. Not only did her table manners shock him, but also what occurred later the same day. He witnessed the beginning of her journey out of the Alzheimer stupor she had deteriorated into. After reading this book I began to wonder if the watermelon episode written about in this chapter, was somehow related. If so, continued research in this direction may one day lead to reversing this dreaded disease.

My feeling is that there is nothing
in life but refraining from hurting others,
and comforting those that are sad.
                                    —Olive Schreiner

CHAPTER EIGHT
The Necessity of Food

When she answered the door, I was greeted by a skeletal figure with flaming red, short-cropped hair. I could not help but stare for a brief moment before introducing myself. I was there to do an assessment for this 81-year-old woman who wished to remain living independently. Her name was Marion and she had been in the hospital with pneumonia. It was obvious by her appearance, that she also wasn't eating regularly. Her eyes were hollow looking, and her petite frame skin and bones.

Marion had no children and was recently widowed. Most of her friends had died or were in nursing homes. She did have a nephew who kept in contact with her, but with health issues of his own, he was limited in his ability to help her. Marion's central problem was that she spent too much time alone and paid no attention to her dietary needs.

Marion met her husband when she was 17 years old. It was 1943 and the country was at war. She was forced to drop out of high school in senior year, to help support her family.

Marion got a job as a salesgirl in a millinery shop. On days that business was slow, Marion tried the fancy hats on, pretending she was a grand dame. Admiring herself in front of the mirror one such day, oversized floppy hat on, she saw the reflection of a tall, handsome boy. He was about her age, and had a huge grin on his face as he watched this tiny frame with a big hat gesticulating to herself. She "saw" a person of rectitude; and he "saw" a wife and best friend. It was the beginning of a love story that lasted sixty-one years.

After her husband's death, Marion became severely depressed and neglectful. Always fashionably dressed and coifed, her clothes now hung limply off her body, her hair dyed a hideous orangey red. Despite her debilitated condition, Marion did not want to give up her townhouse. She wanted help to remain living in the home she and her husband had shared for many years.

Our primary concern for Marion was nutrition. Older bodies require the same amount of nutrients as younger bodies. In home care, we see many seniors who live alone and do not eat a well-balanced meal. They may receive meals on wheels, pick at the food, and then stockpile leftovers in the refrigerator, which end up going rancid. In many cases widowers had a wife who did the bulk of the cooking and now alone, do not know their way around the kitchen. It is also common for elderly to become isolated once children are grown, or a spouse dies. Living alone, they resist preparing a meal for one. A certain percentage of seniors are housebound and cannot get out to buy food. Others, quite simply, don't have enough money. Physical and metabolic changes of the aging body—such as false teeth, poor digestion, natural decline in appetite or sense of taste, pain, and various illnesses—can cause a person to stop eating. We set up a home care plan for Marion that included grocery shopping, meal preparation and socialization. She did not want help with personal care, however we matched her with an aide in the event she needed hands-on care, such as a shampoo. Leslie, Marion's aide, focused on meal preparation and grocery shopping. She made sure to buy plenty of fresh fruits and vegetables every week. Leslie also froze containers of soup for Marion to have advance meals on the weekends. Recognizing that Marion was lonely without her husband and not motivated to prepare and eat meals alone, Leslie suggested to Marion they rearrange her kitchen so she could eat sitting by a window. This way, rather than be in an isolated, darkened corner of the room, Marion could watch what was happening outdoors while she dined. Leslie also tried different recipes, set an attractive table, and put on soft background music. She encouraged her client to seek out new friends in the complex. Gradually, Marion began to take an interest in the world around her again.

Leslie still grocery shops and prepares some advance meals. Marion joined a group of neighborhood women who walk together every day. She also made friends with another widow living in the complex. Once a week they lunch together at a favorite restaurant, dessert included.

With her improved diet, socializing, and regular exercise, we saw a marked improvement in Marion. She updated her wardrobe and chose a more appropriate hair color. On a recent visit, Marion talked excitedly about spending the upcoming holidays with her nephew and his family.

Two roads diverged in a yellow wood,
And sorry I could not travel both
—lines from "The Road Not Taken"
Robert Frost

CHAPTER NINE
Make a Choice

The call comes anytime day or night. An elderly parent has experienced a medical crisis. Once emotions calm and composure is regained, decisions must be made. Unfortunately, most families are not prepared to make long term care choices, because they have neither discussed nor researched viable options beforehand.

Sam lived alone in a single family bungalow. Having resided in this same home and community since 1946, he felt a deep sense of security and bond between neighbors that grew stronger with each passing year. Once a week, at the local diner, Sam shared breakfast and small talk with a group of close friends. These townies, at one time, occupied two or three tables but old age, illness and death took its toll over the years. Nowadays, four remaining friends fit securely into one booth. Following his wife's sudden death in an automobile accident, it was this same group of friends who brought solace to Sam, without using words, but simply by showing up each week. Shortly after the funeral, Jill asked her father to move in with her family. Sam flat out refused. He could not fathom surrendering his home and familiar lifestyle to live in a sprawling, executive development of oversized colonials with multi-car garages and in-ground pools. It still saddened him each time he drove out for a visit, because he remembered the acres of fertile farmland which once contained crops, now filled with blacktop and McMansions. Jill never broached the subject of combining households again.

Six months later, Jill and her husband were enjoying an evening at home with their children, when word came from the hospital that her father, Sam, had fallen on his basement stairs and subsequently drove *himself* to the emergency room. The admitting doctor opted to keep Sam overnight for observation and transfer him to a rehabilitation facility the next morning. Jill was given the name of the facility and the approximate time her father would arrive the following day. Unfamiliar with the sort of questions to ask a hospital discharge planner or that returning home was even an option, Jill proceeded to mentally map out where the facility was located and how much time it might take for her to drive there.

Initially, the rehab facility where her father was sent appeared satisfactory. However, problems emerged soon thereafter. Sam was not receiving the recommended physical therapy. Isolated, he sat moping in his room most of the time. Jill began to realize that if left to languish in this environment, he would never recuperate to the point of being discharged home.

When an aide at the rehab center told Jill about our

agency, she promptly called us and scheduled an in-home assessment. That her father could return home and eventually resume his independent lifestyle was of primary concern to Jill. Together, with Jill and Sam, we discussed the ADL (activities of daily living) tasks needed and put together a home care plan. Oftentimes, home modifications may be required and durable medical equipment needed. With the help of an experienced home care professional, this can be done in a relatively short period of time. In Sam's case, we recommended bathroom grab bars, a shower stool, safety mat, and hand-held shower.

We assigned an aide, Elinore, to this case because in addition to personal care, Sam needed assistance with light housework, laundry, meal preparation and grocery shopping. Elinore's service with Sam began with five mornings a week. As he grew stronger and more independent, service was reduced to three visits per week. Six months later, when Sam was able to resume driving, he no longer needed home care assistance.

Jill was very pleased with the service her dad received and acknowledged that the decision for Sam to voluntarily leave the facility and return home would not have been possible without home care. Both admitted they were remiss in not having had a long term care discussion 'in the event of' and that Sam intended to alert his friends at the diner about the importance of advance preparation.

PART II

After Mary's husband passed away, her son, Robert, tried

to convince her to move in with his family. Not wanting to alter her lifestyle, she refused, choosing instead to relocate to a senior condominium complex. Mary quickly made friends and became active in the community, even daring to love again when she began dating one of her neighbors. When Mary, who turned 78 on her last birthday, began repeating herself and forgetting things Robert assumed it was part of the natural aging process.

A woman with boundless energy, Mary had always been eager to pursue new interests. Marrying young, she had three children by age 25. Totally engaged in motherhood and loving her role, Mary welcomed every opportunity to participate in activities involving her children. The first to volunteer, it didn't matter to Mary whether she was baking cookies, leading a Brownie troop or chaperoning a class of rambunctious elementary school children. After one such trip with her son's fourth grade class to a local sheep farm, where she learned about the shearing, spinning and dyeing of wool, Mary was inspired to learn how to knit. She eventually became quite skilled at the craft. When her children went off to college, Mary decided the time was right to take business courses and turn her dream of owning a small knitting shop into reality. Over the years, her business venture was successful enough for Mary to retire comfortably.

Robert's worries intensified when his mother began responding to junk-mail contests and scam artists on the phone. She also began making errors in her checkbook and experiencing frequent memory lapses. Whenever Robert confronted his mother with these concerns she became belligerent and accused Robert of trying to take his inheritance before she was dead. All conversation abruptly ceased and the remainder of his visit was strained.

The crisis call came on a Saturday afternoon. Robert's mother had been in a car accident. After a week in the hospital, Mary was transferred to a rehab unit for physical therapy. Robert received more bad news from the rehab facility. Attempting to go to the bathroom in the middle of the night and being in a strange place, Mary became disoriented, fell and suffered head trauma. Mary required emergency surgery. Over the next few weeks her condition deteriorated. Following a second surgery, Mary was placed in the critical care unit, where she passed away.

Robert was despondent. He experienced tremendous guilt about his decision to have his mother transferred to the rehab center instead of taking her home. Robert had called our agency to inquire about home care when his mother was in the hospital following her auto accident. However, he lacked sufficient time to adequately consider this option. Many individuals in the midst of a medical crisis, are unfamiliar with home care as an alternative to custodial placement. The message communicated is that when a discharge is delayed, costs increase, as well as the risk of placement in a less suitable facility. Patients and family members are overwhelmed with medical terminology, diagnosis, prognosis and the fact that most people are now discharged 'quicker and sicker.' Overwhelmed by the thought of becoming sole caretaker, panic takes hold which, in turn, leads to rash, poorly thought out decisions.

If the family had considered home care Robert's mother could have recuperated at her son's home until she was able to resume living independently in her condominium. Basic safety modifications would have been made, and durable medical equipment purchased. Obtaining a shower chair and hand-held unit enables a client to enjoy a shower rather than a sponge bath. If grab bars are not already in place in the bath area, they can be installed quickly with a clamp-on model, and then easily removed if no longer needed. As part of Mary's home care plan, we would have assisted Robert in both identifying and meeting these needs.

In those instances where home care is feasible, our agency staff begins work immediately so that service can begin upon hospital discharge. Throughout the initial assessment, we address any questions or concerns a prospective client may have, so that a viable plan of care can be put in place. Should a client be receiving a visiting nurse for a few weeks after hospital discharge, we may initially assign a homemaker. After the nursing service ends, we add the personal care component. Follow-up phone calls and supervisory visits are made regularly. Just as it is wise to seek a second medical opinion, home care should always be explored as an option and every effort made, after a medical crisis, to return an individual to their familiar home environment.

Sometimes it is the artist's task to find out how much music you can still make with what you have left.

—Itzhak Perlman

CHAPTER TEN
An Unpredictable Disease

Multiple Sclerosis (MS) is a disease of the central nervous system. Unpredictable in terms of severity and progression, most often, it strikes individuals in their 20s, 30s & 40s. If home care is not promoted as a viable option for the MS patient who is diagnosed before the age of forty, the result could be many years of adult life spent in custodial care.

We received a call from the daughter of a former employee. Her roommate from college, now in her twenties, was diagnosed with MS. Barely out of school, en route to a successful career, the young girl was stricken by a disease that has begun to affect younger victims.

When our agency nurse made her initial home visit to Linda, she was met by a petite, attractive woman of 28. Before setting up a formal care plan, they sat down and reviewed Linda's medical history. Linda was working full-time at her dream job and too busy to pay attention to her body's warning signs. She went on to say, "it was not the tingling sensations or muscle spasms, but the extreme fatigue that finally forced me to a doctor and ultimately the diagnosis of MS."

When first told she had MS, Linda became very depressed, quit her job, and alienated most of her family and friends. With counseling and the help of the local MS support group, Linda finally began accepting the chronic nature of her condition. She confided how difficult it was to live with a disease that can go into remission and then relapse. There are times in remission when patients look and feel well. People question why a relatively young person is using a handicapped space when they appear perfectly healthy. Along with accepting the limitations associated with progressive MS, Linda had to assume responsibility for managing her health, taking medications, and seeking outside help when needed.

We matched Linda with Tess, a caregiver experienced with MS patients. Her care plan was set up to provide assistance with housework, laundry, grocery shopping and necessary errands. Linda realized that, although she did not require assistance with meals at this time, as the disease progressed, she might need help with feeding. People with MS frequently develop swallowing disorders and need a patient caregiver who does not become tense and upset, as this can cause the client to also tense up and choke. Linda was struggling with bouts of depression and inappropriate emotional responses—again, byproducts of the insidious disease. Her physician had prescribed new medication and early results were promising. Linda needed a caregiver who would not become flustered or personalize her inappropriate emotional response, if she cried at something happy or did not cry at something sad.

Tess paid particular attention to any skin changes, because frequently individuals with MS cannot feel when they bump themselves or receive a cut. Tess also monitored Linda if she appeared more fatigued than usual as this could signal impending infection. It is so important for a good match between client and caregiver because, through regular interaction, a skilled caregiver will notice emotional and physical changes and immediately report them to an agency supervisor.

MS symptoms can be exacerbated by heat and humidity. For this reason, Tess was always prepared with compresses in the freezer. Knowing that Linda experienced short-term memory loss, Tess kept a keen eye on Linda's appointment calendar. Homemakers and aides do not get involved with a client's finances or personal matters, however, they can remind a client of scheduled doctor visits and medication regimens. Oftentimes a client's aide will be asked by a family member to assist with personal grooming on the day of an appointment.

One of the hardest changes Linda had to cope with was her social life. Prior to her diagnosis, she was, by her own description, a social butterfly. She kept in touch with friends back to elementary school in the small Midwestern town where she grew up. And as a single, attractive young woman, she enjoyed a busy social life. Multiple Sclerosis changed all that! Linda ended friendships with those who thought she looked too good to be sick and should be able to keep up with their marathon shopping weekends. She also became more selective with male friends, learning the hard way that it takes a special person to date someone with limitations.

More than once, she had to cancel a date at the last minute because of extreme fatigue.

Tess and Linda had an excellent relationship, not only as caregiver and client, but also on a deeper, personal level. Tess had gone through a life-altering personal tragedy and relocated here from a large metropolitan city seven years earlier. She rebuilt her professional and personal life without the close support of family and friends. Linda felt that she and Tess bonded so readily because they both experienced major upheavals in their life and learned how to cope with the changes. Linda takes one day at a time and is thankful for the assistance she receives from Tess because in her words, "If it wasn't for Tess, I couldn't live independently at home."

My problem was I could never figure out how to
build anything with just one side to it.
There can't be good without bad, life without
death, pleasure without pain.
That's the way it is. If I take sad away,
happy has to go with it."
—Oh God! Book II (1980)

CHAPTER ELEVEN
Flexibility A Must

A diagnosis of cancer is still the most dreaded and feared of all possible illnesses. It is the second leading cause of death for adults, and the older one gets, chances of cancer increase. Everyone has been touched by this disease, if not directly then by knowing of someone with cancer. The good news is that more people are living with and surviving cancer. The downside is that treatment interrupts daily routine and patients experience negative side effects such as nausea, fatigue, poor nutrition and oftentimes depression.

Over the years, we at Ideal Home Care have provided service to many cancer patients. There will be days when treatment is prolonged, delayed, or just overwhelming for the patient, forcing them to cancel their home care service on short notice. Subsequently, flexible scheduling is a must. We make every effort to reschedule the home care component for a more convenient time. This, as well, is a stressful period for family members. Everyone has to accept and come to terms with the disease and prognosis. Decisions must be made regarding a treatment plan, living arrangements, transportation needs, and daily care. In addition to physical stress, there is a great deal of emotional duress.

Prior to matching an aide or homemaker with a cancer patient, we learn as much as we can about the family and their role in assisting the client through this crisis. Having home care service during cancer treatment not only assists an individual to remain in their home, but also provides valuable support to family members involved in patient care. A homemaker can do light housework such as vacuuming, dusting, washing floors and keeping a client's living space neat and clean. They will also change bed linens as often as needed, do laundry, grocery shop and pick up prescriptions. A client who needs assistance with personal care will be matched with an aide. Clients often report how much better they feel after a shower and shampoo, and greatly appreciate receiving early morning personal care on the days they are scheduled for treatment.

Good nutrition is particularly important for a cancer patient. There will be times during treatment when a client has little or no appetite. Our homemakers and aides will prepare nutritious meals in advance, and leave them for later consumption. They adhere to all dietary needs/restrictions listed on the client care plan. They also report changes in eating habits, sleep disturbances, mood changes and overall well-being.

Throughout the year we offer continuing education

classes, given by a volunteer from the American Cancer Society, on a specific cancer topic. These workshops ensure that our homemakers and aides are kept current on new treatments and studies. For example, recent research indicates that physical exercise during treatment and recovery can improve quality of life and psychological well-being of a patient. Knowing this, our caregivers will encourage clients to remain physically active.

We at Ideal Home Care have seen the survival rate for cancer patients increase over the past thirty years. I personally believe a key factor is the ability to remain at home during the treatment and recovery period. A crucial time for cancer patients, it is extremely important to have the security and comfort of home, surrounded by all that is familiar.

Sweet is the smile of home;
the mutual look
When hearts are of each other sure;
Sweet all the joys that crowd
the household nook,
The haunts of all affections pure.

—John Keble

CHAPTER TWELVE
Pushed and Pulled

The fundamental building block of society is the family. And growing old should be considered a privilege where one is revered within family and society. Words from former UN Secretary General Kofi Annan say it best:

"Trees grow stronger over the years, rivers wider. Likewise, with age, human beings gain immeasurable depth and breadth of experience and wisdom. That is why older persons should be not only respected and revered, they should be utilized as the rich resource to society that they are."

However, more often than not, aging is met with resistance, discomfort and fear. Many seniors dread the thought of no longer being able to care for themselves and having to "be placed" in a nursing home or other institutionalized care, to live out the remainder of their days amongst strangers. Although most families resist this option, if they are not aware of alternatives, placement becomes their *only* choice. Institutional care can cause strife within the family unit, especially if the placement is made with trepidation or falls short of everyone's expectation. There is nothing more heart-wrenching than to enter a parent's assisted living apartment and find one's mother or father sitting alone in darkness. Whether the cause be a broken light bulb or the inability to flick a switch, the results are the same—a loved one alone, frightened and confused.

Seniors at home rather than in a custodial care setting live longer and have a better quality of life. A person choosing home care has a voice in money spent because they can control the number of service hours received. Also, there is more flexibility to tailor the plan of care to each client's specific needs. And other family members can be involved as much as desired. Unlike nursing homes or assisted living facilities, it is not an "all or nothing" type of service where one relinquishes control of their finances and individualism in exchange for round-the-clock care that may be unnecessary. Unfortunately, these home care statistics and facts are not common knowledge. Most callers to our agency are unfamiliar with home care, do not know where to begin, and are usually in crisis. The following represents a typical call to our agency and the procedure we use to assist the caller.

Stephanie B. is a 44-year-old wife, mother and daughter living a hectic lifestyle regimented by the moving hands of the clock. Starting her day at 5:00 A.M., she rouses her three children and readies them for school. By 7:30 once her husband and children are out the door, Stephanie jumps in the shower, more to fully waken than cleanse. At 9:00 upstairs in her home office, she places orders for colored fabrics, paints and swatches, configures designs and schedules appointments - all tasks involved with her interior decorating business. Breaking for lunch at noontime, Stephanie also calls her 77-year-old mother for a wellness check and medication reminder. By 2:00 P.M. Stephanie must be finished with her design work and begin shuttling the kids to after-school activities. She also has to prepare the evening meal. Before retiring to bed for the night, Stephanie will check tomorrow's calendar in the event her mother needs transportation to a medical appointment.

Stephanie is part of the "sandwich generation." In addition to ministering to her own family, she is also overseeing her mother's needs. Stephanie knows that her mother wants to continue living independently in the community, and will do everything she can to help fulfill that wish. Stephanie's Dad died in a nursing home, and both she and her mother vowed they would never go through such a clinically sterile experience again, yet, they never sat down and discussed a long term care plan or what they would do in the event of a medical emergency.

The third week in October while closing her garden for the season, her mother tripped over a rake and ended up with a broken arm. Stephanie was in crisis! She knew that her mother could not prepare meals, perform any personal care or other daily living tasks without assistance. Stephanie could not put her life on hold for the several weeks it would take for her mother to mend. Stephanie does not know what home care is nor how to begin the process of keeping her mother home.

Stephanie began researching options on the internet, asking friends' advice and thumbing through the yellow pages randomly, phoning home health care agencies. She soon learned that it would cost approximately $279.00/day for nursing home care versus an average of $23.00/hour for in-home care. When Stephanie called our agency, we did not just try to sell her our service. We gave her enough information, with varying options, so that she was able to make an informed decision on how best to keep her mother at home.

In similar situations, either our geriatric care specialist or staff nurse will make a free in-home assessment. Many prospective clients know they do not require round-the-clock care but are not sure how much time is needed to be maintained at home, or if any durable medical equipment as well as home modifications might be necessary. The home care service plan that we arranged for Stephanie's mother began with two hours daily, Monday through Friday to assist with personal care and all daily living tasks. The local meals-on-wheels delivered hot and nutritious lunches. Stephanie stopped by every evening to ready her mother for bed. This service continued until Stephanie's mom had her cast removed, at which time a re-assessment of needs was done.

Stephanie's mother was anxious to resume some of her light housework tasks and to prepare her own meals. She also was able to do personal grooming again. We decreased the service to two hours twice a week for assistance with laundry, vacuuming and grocery shopping. When Stephanie was comfortable enough with her mother resuming a fully independent lifestyle, she terminated home care service. Stephanie was very pleased with the care her mother received, which not only allowed recuperation at home, but also was invaluable for Stephanie, who otherwise would have had to put her own family life on hold. Oftentimes, home care benefits immediate family members as well as client; as in this case, rather than Stephanie becoming stressed to the max finding sufficient time to meet the needs of her own nuclear family as well as an aging parent, an aide/homemaker can relieve an overwhelmed family member.

. . . that moment between the bud and the rose
is only known to those that become roses
—excerpt from a Sufi writing

CHAPTER THIRTEEN
Lifetime Commitment

I remember a visit to my parents, finding them both in the kitchen attempting to thread a needle. My mother held the needle as my father tried to feed thread through the eye. Intervening, I finished the task within seconds but realized afterwards that, left alone, they would have succeeded in their task *together.* They were two individuals functioning as one. Having been married nearly sixty years, my parents had a special bond—the kind that can only exist between two people who have spent the better part of a lifetime together, the kind that cannot be comprehended by anyone who has not experienced it.

The greatest challenge confronting couples desiring to remain together at home after a medical crisis generally comes from their adult children. They will advocate for institutional care when one parent becomes ill or disabled, reasoning that to assume the caregiver role will become a burden for the healthier parent. The fact that their parents want to stay together—even expected the time would come when one of them would fall ill—is never considered.

The possibility exists for couples to remain together in

their home, but advance planning is necessary. Home care service can successfully assist couples with this choice, however family members must be made aware early on. Frequently, only following medical crisis is the option to stay home voiced, but this is also a time when couples are most vulnerable. Patient and family are too overwhelmed to research the home care process.

Home care service can be set up for both, or if one spouse is needier, the more independent of the two may require respite time. An in-home assessment is usually done to assist with a service plan. Suggestions are given regarding safety issues and home modifications that will make a couple's service more effective. Simple modifications that can be done include adding grab bars to tub and shower enclosures, turning down the hot water temperature to prevent scalding and keeping pathways free of obstructions to avoid accidents.

Home care for couples is not only feasible but also cost effective. In 2011 the national average cost for a private nursing home room was $239.00/day with the highest rate in Alaska at $655.00/day and the lowest in Louisiana at $141.00/day. The average national rate for a home health aide was $21.00 /hour and a homemaker cost $19.00/hour. Recipients have a say in how many service hours they receive and know the total cost well in advance. There are no *hidden* fees. Couples do not have to relinquish control of their assets along with their independence. A care plan is tailored to specific needs, precluding services they may not require. In the future the care plan can be modified accordingly.

We at Ideal Home Care fully realize that couples build a distinctive history and years of shared memories. As aging produces visible changes—graying hair, wrinkling skin, arthritic limbs—so too comes the partnered strength to endure what comes with this passage of time. Life partners bolster each other as they pass through life's stages. The reassurance of an embrace in the dark; a look that speaks volumes; healing laughter—these subtle nuances represent the sum of all that makes two individuals become like one. Growing old is challenge enough without the added fear of separation and being forced to finish life's journey alone. Assisted living facilities and nursing homes are structured to accommodate individuals, not couples. Once the choice to remain at home is made, our goal as home care professionals is to work with couples, assisting them to live out their remaining days *together.*

*Love is the emblem of eternity; it
confounds all notion of time; effaces
all memory of a beginning, all fear of an end.*

—Madame de Stael

CHAPTER FOURTEEN
Twin Souls

The first lesson learned in Psychology 101 is never get personally involved with a client. But if someone like Alice comes into your life, this rule is rendered optional. Alice and Gabe T were the first couple to receive home care service from our agency. After nearly seven decades together, they still shared a deep-rooted love for each other.

Gabe and Alice met in high school. He was 17 and she 15. He liked sports. She read the classics. Both of Jewish descent, they lived in Dorchester. It was early 1900s and the three-tenement houses of this Boston suburb were inhabited by growing numbers of European immigrants. Despite the fact that Alice's parents thought she was too young to be on the receiving end of Gabe's affections, she never doubted— "marrying this handsome and wonderful guy." After graduating high school Gabe immediately went to work full time in his father's haberdashery to save enough money for marriage. Gabe and Alice wed in 1912 and moved into the third-floor apartment of his father's house. They intended to start a family and buy a home of their own. "God had other plans," Alice said and, in the absence of children of their own, the couple shared their love with nieces and nephews.

When I met Gabe and Alice they were inquiring about home care because Gabe had recently been discharged from the hospital coronary unit. I spent a great deal of time with them during our first visit, allowing Gabe and Alice to share their story. Alice needed someone patient with her speech. She had suffered a stroke the year before, and although she worked long and hard with a therapist, still had difficulty speaking. When anxious, she became unintelligible, and would resort to gesticulating and using an impromptu sign language. Knowing how determined Alice was to improve her communication skills, Gabe coached her, using flash cards and reading books aloud as she followed along.

This couple desperately wanted to remain together in their home, but were hesitant to ask extended family for help, fearing they would be forced into a nursing home, or worse yet, *separated*! They had never been apart from each other with the exception of recent hospitalizations.

Early in their marriage, when Alice did not become pregnant, neither blamed the other nor did they ever consider ending the marriage. Gabe explained that, if anything, infertility brought them closer. Alice confided, "Life's a *mitzvah,* a blessing. We're in this together—the up's and down's—'til the end."

Genuine twin souls, this couple was truly devoted to each other. With our conversation finished, Gabe and Alice stood up to escort me out. Reflexively as a breath, their hands reached out to meet each other and linked together. Theirs was an infectious love that spread to all who came in contact.

I left their home determined to keep Gabe and Alice together.

Because they needed split shift care – morning and evening, as well as weekend service - Gabe and Alice were matched with more than one caregiver. Both received personal care early in the morning. Homemaker tasks were done later in the day followed by evening meal prep. When scheduling split-shift, combined service, an aide is assigned for the A.M. personal care, and a homemaker takes care of the household tasks and meal preparations. Gabe and Alice were pleased with all their caregivers and grateful to be able to remain together in their home.

Less than a year into the service, Gabe suffered a fatal heart attack. Overcome with grief, Alice took comfort in the fact that they were together until the end. Still determined to remain in her own home, we continued with personal care and homemaker service. Although Alice was receiving excellent care and her home was spotless, we professionals can lose sight of the fact that loneliness and grief can linger. Several times a week I called Alice and did a wellness check over the phone. On my last supervisory home visit, she behaved in a detached manner. Previously exuberant and engaging, Alice appeared serene and peaceful. She talked about having no regrets in life and the importance of being at peace with oneself before death. This woman of immigrant ancestry with barely a high school education demonstrated such wisdom! As always, we parted with a hug but this time Alice added a 'Thank you for everything," and an extra long embrace. In retrospect I am certain she sensed it would be our last time together. Soon thereafter Alice died in her sleep.

I missed Alice deeply but was consoled by the fact that, with our home care service, Gabe and Alice were able to keep the vow they made to each other decades earlier—"till death do we part."

The lesson I gleaned from this experience is the importance of always considering home care for couples rather than separating them after shared years of life and love. Two people who have lived together for many years truly become as one. The decision to end this partnership should never be imposed on them. Once home care is chosen, it is our job to determine how best to keep a couple together at home.

How do geese know when to fly to the sun?
Who tells them the seasons?
How do we, humans, know when it is time to
move on? As with the migrant
birds, so surely with us, there is a voice
within, if only we would listen to it,
that tells us so certainly when to go forth into
the unknown.

—Elizabeth Kubler-Ross

CHAPTER FIFTEEN
Death is Not Optional

When I was a child, I would ask my father what death was like. He simply responded that dying was like going to sleep. As I grew older, I of course realized that death was not that simple. A person dying of a terminal illness could linger before death finally comes; or one might die suddenly, leaving behind a great deal unfinished. In the former, there is time for closure, while in the latter those left behind oftentimes suffer endless guilt for lack of closure.

I have committed my professional career to keeping individuals at home. A growing concern in this country is the lack of government funding for home-based, long term care. When individuals are no longer able to care for themselves, they should not be forced out of their homes where all is familiar, and become part of a system that strips away independence and dignity. In *The Adult Years,* philosopher Lin Yutang writes, "The symphony of life should end with a grand finale of peace and serenity and material comfort and spiritual contentment, and not with the crash of a broken drum or cracked cymbals."

The phone call was the first to come in on a Monday morning. It was from a client's daughter and we could tell from the sound of her voice that she was crying. Her mother, our client for the past eight years, had passed away Sunday afternoon. She wanted to be sure we notified her mother's aide, and also needed a comforting ear while she grieved. She was consoled by the fact that her mother's wish to die at home, with family at bedside, had been fulfilled. Years before, when her father became ill, the family felt powerless against a medical system that took over. He died in a nursing home without family present. Rather, the only person was a cantankerous roommate who constantly yelled and fussed with the knobs on his radio. They felt endless guilt, holding onto the thought that their loved one's last moments were tainted by this individual's high-pitched shrill voice and crackling radio static.

Oftentimes, family will struggle with the decision whether to keep their loved one at home or place them in a nursing home. Children, who now are the caregiver for parents, find the reversed role difficult to accept. And when their parent is dying, emotions can affect judgment, rendering decision making all the more arduous. Home care service assists individuals to remain at home with dignity until end of life. Even a client who is no longer ambulatory can have a plan of care tailored to individual needs whereby a skilled aide will give a sponge bath, hair grooming, and oral hygiene as well as change the bed linens without having to transfer the client from his sick bed. The bond that is formed between aide and client can become so strong, that oftentimes, immediate family will request the aide's presence during the last hours of a client's life.

We are a society that shuns death, as though to deny it will prevent it from happening. In the early part of the twentieth century the vast majority of people died at home surrounded by family. A doctor routinely made house visits and his primary role was to alleviate pain and suffering. Today, our elderly die in institutions surrounded, not by loved ones, but rather by unfamiliar sights, antiseptic smells and the whirring sounds of medical technology. In his book, *Last Rights,* Stephen Kiernen says so strikingly "death is only an instant—it's what comes before that is important." There have been numerous reports of elderly nursing home patients receiving inadequate pain medication, which leaves them distressed and in unnecessary pain during this time before death.

Medical advances make it possible to treat and prolong life, hence, most of our elderly clients with chronic illnesses will live longer. However, this does not mean that home care will be chosen over institutional care, due in large part to economics. More individuals die in hospitals and nursing homes because the bill is being paid by the government. Managed care tries to avoid the dying patient. Even the Medicare hospice benefit, which does cover services at home, is designated for the patient generally determined by their physician to be in a failure to thrive state, expected to live less than six months. What was once a natural part of the life cycle changed with the availability of a place to send your old, sick family member to die and the government paying for it.

In our thirty years of providing home care service, many of our clients have died at home. But there have also been too many in my opinion that were *never given that choice*. If you want to keep your chronically ill loved one at home, no payment system presently exists to assist you. Medicare covers home care for a brief period of time when an individual discharged from a hospital or rehabilitation facility needs skilled nursing. When skilled nursing is no longer required, the home care visits terminate. You must pay out of pocket for services or qualify for Medicaid, city/state programs or local charities, all of which are already strained in today's dismal economic climate. Government sponsored health care reform needs to include paid services for our growing elderly population who wish to remain at home. If federal and state policy makers refuse to do the math and see that home care is a more cost-effective choice, preferable over nursing homes, then we will remain an institutional biased society—awaiting, as Lin Yutang so eloquently infers, the grand finale of broken drums and cracked cymbals.

When an old man dies, a library burns down
                                    —African proverb

CHAPTER SIXTEEN
A Full Life

Jack T. died today. For ten years prior to his passing, he received service from our agency and, for all those years, was cared for by the same aide, Tom. Jack lived alone, but was never lonely for he had a host of hobbies and outside interests.

His birth name was Armando. Common for young people born at the turn of the century to change their name to a more American one, he preferred Jack. His father died when he was a young boy. To help care for their widowed mother, Jack and his older brother went to work. He sold newspapers on the street corners of the growing capital city, while his brother began a career in the jewelry industry.

Shortly after Jack's brother married and relocated to New York City, tragedy struck. Leaving work late one evening, his brother was mugged. While trying to fight off the attackers, he fell, hit his head on the curb and died in the hospital a few days later. Within the same year, Jack's mother, broken hearted over the loss of her son, also passed away. At the time, Jack was engaged to marry but overwhelming grief catapulted him into a depression. Abandoning plans to marry and settle down, he decided instead to leave the state, and for years thereafter lived a bohemian lifestyle. Losing his immediate family at such a young age taught Jack the importance of friendship. Throughout his life he cherished and nurtured a close circle of confidants with letters, phone calls and visits.

Jack eventually returned to this area to live out the remainder of his life, with the intent of being interred next to his mother, father and brother. He settled into a luxury apartment in Providence, which put him within walking distance of his two favorite pastimes—reading and music. Jack played cornet for many years in community orchestras. When he no longer possessed the lung power to perform in public, he still kept his silver-plated French Besson cornet, oiled and freshly polished, in his bedroom closet. Reading was a part of Jack's daily routine. He would spend hours at the library, returning home with an armful of books.

Macular Degeneration prompted Jack to contact our agency. His loss of vision made it nearly impossible for him to read and keep up the daily care of his apartment. Jack's service began with two and a half hours a week. In addition to light housework, Tom's duties included reading historical non-fiction to Jack and keeping him abreast of current events.

Over the decade, Jack's health deteriorated, resulting in a need for additional services. Because Tom was an aide, he added personal care to his homemaker duties, assisting Jack with a shower and making sure that his full head of white hair was always well groomed. As the years passed, a special bond developed between caregiver and client. Jack enjoyed describing to Tom the various parts of the country he had lived in and the numerous interesting adventures experienced. Jack painted a picture of contrast for Tom as he spoke of the poverty in Appalachia versus the wealth of Hollywood, the rural plains of Kansas as opposed to the jazzy glamour of Las Vegas.

The summer months proved very difficult for Jack this year. Now nearly blind and suffering a severe heart condition, he began deteriorating rapidly. By summer's end, Jack was bedridden. Having no immediate family, he confided to Tom his wish and determination to die at home, dignity intact. Jack instructed Tom to arrange his most memorable photos on the bed-side table. He also listened to his special brass band and classical music each afternoon and into the evening. In addition to his favorite sights and sounds, Jack wanted to be surrounded by his own smells, known as occupant odor. These are the various odors that are in everyone's home. They are a blend of all the different products we use each day such as soaps, perfumes, cleaning supplies, cooking herbs, even odors from a fireplace or wood burning stove. Most people cannot smell their own home, but *do* notice, when visiting someone else's house, the uniquely distinct smell. Jack felt comfortable and at peace in his home. Anticipating the end was near, Jack's visiting nurse was at his home every day, and Tom increased his time to seven days per week. Drifting in and out of consciousness, Jack was still able to recognize and attempt a weak response to the sound of Tom's voice.

Jack T. died this afternoon. Tom was at his bedside, providing gentle care, as Jack passed peacefully.

An elderly patient visits his doctor complaining about pain in his right knee. The doctor examines the knee and says "At your age, Joe, you've got to expect things like this. You're not as young as you were, you know." "But doctor, explain something to me" replies Joe. "My left knee is just as old as my right knee but it doesn't hurt at all!"

CHAPTER SEVENTEEN
Laughter Is The Best Medicine

No one can tell a story like Harry. I think he embellishes a bit, but just loves to hear you laugh. I always know when Harry is on the phone with one of the office employees, because the sound of laughter resonates throughout the building, as he recounts one of his latest adventures. My personal favorite dates back to his youth:

"It was during Prohibition. My father made his own beer, wine and the occasional bottle of whiskey, which was only taken out when the men got together to play cards. It was a wintry night, the family was in bed and my mother heard the crunch of snow under heavy footsteps. Instinctively, she bolts out of bed, grabs the whiskey and stuffs it into her feather mattress that were common in those

79

days. There's a hasty rap on the door and in barge two Prohibition agents. They begin searching the entire house! My mother and father are panicked. My siblings and I were told to stay in our beds and be quiet (which we did!) These two guys were looking so hard to find that bottle of whiskey that one of them sits down on a crate of beer to flash his light under the pantry sink. So certain was he of finding that whiskey under the sink that he never noticed the beer under the seat of his pants!"

Harry is a high energy, "Type A personality." After retiring from a successful career in retail sales, he "downsized" from his three bedroom home in an executive neighborhood, to an adults only condominium complex. Harry soon became active in the condo housing association, and organized trips for the residents. He also joined a local theatre group, fulfilling a life-long dream to perform on stage. He preferred comedies, and his favorite role was playing Oscar in Neil Simon's *The Odd Couple.* Everyone that Harry met became an immediate friend and receiver of his many jokes. As the years passed, Harry slowed down physically but remained mentally astute.

At age 86, needing a walker to ambulate, Harry gave up driving. That is when he became a client of ours. He needed weekly grocery shopping and necessary errands. One of his many friends at the local senior center told him about our agency.

Harry initially contracted for home care service one day a week. Now at age 93, and increasingly frail, Harry receives two days per week to include meal preps and laundry. Harry retains the ability to laugh! He still opens every conversation with a humorous anecdote. Never a complainer, he only laments feeling more isolated, having outlived all his closest friends. "The best days of the week," he says, "are Tuesday and Thursday when my homemaker, Essie, comes." Essie is the perfect match for Harry, because in addition to her excellent home care skills, she too has a great sense of humor. She never tires of Harry's funny stories and recollections of his youth.

Essie is at Harry's condo two hours on Tuesdays for meal prep and laundry. She changes the bed linens and puts his clothes in the washer. She then prepares Harry's breakfast. While he is eating, Essie switches the clothes into the dryer. After Harry finishes with breakfast, they discuss current events while she cleans the kitchen. Because Harry does not get out much anymore, he calls Essie "his window to the world." Our professional term is *socialization.* Many of our clients look forward to chatting with their homemaker or aide. For this reason, we encourage our caregivers to engage in conversation. For those clients with a busy enough life, we keep socialization off the care plan. On Thursdays Essie provides three hours of homemaker service. After preparing Harry's breakfast, she is off to the market. When she returns, Harry is waiting to chat with her while she puts the groceries away. Once a month Essie adds a trip to the local pharmacy to pick up refills on Harry's medication.

Harry is proof enough for us that a positive outlook adds years and vitality to life. Harry will tell you he has no regrets. And if he had to do it all over again, he would not change anything, except perhaps keep a journal of all his adventures, because he now has to ask Essie how some of his stories end. He forgets! Harry intends to die at home, preferably asleep in bed after watching an old re-run of a favorite comedy sitcom - *The Honeymooners*, starring Jackie Gleason.

*"The sun setting is no less beautiful
than the sun rising."*
—Chinese Proverb

CHAPTER EIGHTEEN
A Reverence for Nature

The rustic New England farm house, set back from the road, overlooked fields that once were fertile, but now overgrown with weeds. A big red barn, in disrepair, carried a cow-design weathervane on its cupola, giving proof that at one time this was a working farm. Next to the barn sat a vacant chicken coop, tilted precariously to one side. Our geriatric care specialist was called here to give an in-home assessment for Madeleine, a 97-year-old woman, who lived alone on this farm. The case was unusual because no medical crisis occurred beforehand. Madeleine's daughter, Katherine, simply stated that her mother was elderly, not ill, and needed help with personal care.

Following introductions, Katherine began the conversation in a defensive tone. She knew only too well, that on first impression, a 97-year-old woman living alone on an isolated rural farm appeared to be neglected. But to help us understand, Katherine shared a brief portion of her mother's past. Her parents operated a successful dairy farm, supplying milk to homes throughout the rural area. They were well-known in the community for lending a helping hand to a neighboring farmer, volunteering at church and the grange, and Madeleine's apple pies, which always took home a prize ribbon from the local fair. At this point, Madeleine interrupted with a story of her own, recounting how the milk was always bottled raw until the state passed a law requiring the milk be pasteurized. All their cows had to be tested for illnesses that could possibly be transferred to humans. Sick cows were destroyed—they had one put down. Her husband then had to purchase pasteurization equipment. After milking, the raw contents was poured into the machine, pasteurized and then transferred to milk cans that sat on refrigerated flooring.

The conversation then returned to Katherine who stated that, as a family of farmers, they had great reverence for nature—its nurturing as well as destructive capability. And just as each spring the planted seeds sprout life, go through their cycle and die upon winter's arrival, so it is with human life. Her mother had lived a full productive life. The family would let nature take its course, confident that Madeleine would die at home, in her own bed. To emphasize her point further, Katherine explained about the yellow-rumped warbler, a bird that migrates north each year, flying approximately six thousand miles, to builds its nest, more often than not, in the same tree as the year before. Knowing this, why should her mother, now old and widowed, be expected to *leave* "the nest" she had lived in all her life, and build a new one amongst strangers with whom she shared no history or memories. Madeleine's life story resides here in this farming community. Here, her children began life, and here her husband's ended. Walking back from the barn after finishing morning chores, he died of a heart attack before reaching the back door. That was nearly twenty years ago and Madeleine still feels his presence each time she walks the path to the barn, sits at the table they both ate from, sleeps in the same bed they shared for over fifty-five years. She feels the same about her children. Although now grown and living away from the farm, the memories of their birth and youth linger here with Madeleine. She wants to remain in her home and has the support of three generations to help make it happen.

A large boned woman, slightly stooped with osteoarthritis, Madeleine still ambulated without a cane or walker. She was fiercely independent, refusing meals-on-wheels, preferring her own home cooked food. And she rarely used the clothes dryer. On sunny days she would hang the laundry outdoors to dry and bleach in the sun. She kept a clean and uncluttered home.

Madeleine's primary health concern was urinary incontinence, requiring her to wear Depends. Because of her age and osteoarthritis, she was unable to walk quickly, and would lose bladder control before reaching the bathroom. She was self-conscious about her personal hygiene and needed assistance with bathing.

We matched Madeleine with Diana, an aide who lived in the area and was familiar with an agrarian lifestyle. The aide arrived early each morning, for Madeleine was habitually up by dawn, and assisted with a shower and personal grooming. Because Madeleine needed her bed sheets changed and laundered more often, Diana helped with laundry. Madeleine still maintained a daily schedule of household chores and did not want Diana to interfere with this routine. Her family supported this independent stance, recognizing that something as mundane as baking a pan of corn bread gave the older woman purpose and fostered mental clarity. In addition to personal care and laundry assistance, Diana regularly took Madeleine outdoors for walks. The older woman well understood the healing power of nature. Realizing that her agrarian way was becoming extinct, she wanted to share her knowledge of the outdoors and web of life. She would call attention to the sound of a woodpecker or the quick scurry of a chipmunk, and explain that a shift in the weathervane indicated a sudden change in wind direction or an impending storm.

During one of our continuing education classes, Diana shared with the group that working with Madeleine, she realized the importance of everyday rituals. When interrupted, confusion, fear and depression can occur. If temporary, the body and mind can re-adapt but once permanent, such as institutionalization, an individual usually declines to an irreversible state. Diana also shared a second revelation with us: the significance of having a family discussion beforehand, in order to have a plan in place for "when the time comes."

Madeleine's family accepted death for what it is—part of the life cycle. Letting nature take its course, death would come for this 97-year-old matriarch, as it had for previous generations. She knew the bed she would die in, surrounded by all that's familiar. This family of four generations shared a true agrarian kinship.

Observe the life by cause and consequence
Explore the life by wisdom
Treat the life by equality
Complete the life by love

—Buddha

CHAPTER NINETEEN
Secrets of Longevity

On intake, the average age of our geriatric clients is mid-80s. Based on thirty years of experience caring for seniors, it has become readily apparent that the body begins a more rapid decline after the age of 80. However, from this target point, one can remain living independently at home for fifteen to twenty years or more. Genes play an important role in longevity. But one cannot ignore nutrition, mobility, pre-existing medical conditions, and attitude as important factors.

Collected over the years, we at Ideal Home Care share the following 'secrets to a long life':

❖ Those who keep moving stay moving longer; one client was still taking the bus at 99 years of age. Volunteer, tutor at a local school, participate at your local senior center, garden, (my mom, in her late-80s, still continues to plant a vegetable garden each spring); walk every day (I have a neighbor who gave up driving years ago and at 90 is still walking every day, rain or shine). We learned that it is important to stay involved in the world around you and to remain purpose-driven.

❖ Never neglect nutrition. We covered the importance of nutrition in a previous chapter, but it bears repeating that our bodies are fueled by food. Proper nutrition keeps the body well-tuned and running longer. Many of our clients eat *less* as they age, but they do not skip meals, eating their largest meal in the afternoon, and light snacks into the evening. They *do* eat sweets—many eat chocolate on a regular basis; one client of 92 confided that she ate a Twinkie every night.

❖ Family, community and the importance of traditions are often cited - from local grange or church suppers to the weekly family gatherings for dinner and conversation.

❖ Dermatologists will tell you that heredity plays a key role in how your face will age, but *Oil of Olay* is the beauty product used by most of our clients who have the least wrinkles and noticeably radiant skin.

❖ By far, those who can accept all the ups & downs of life and go with the flow, even suffer the most intense grief—the loss of a child—frequently live well into their 90s and require the least amount of home care hours. These clients also have a strong religious faith that sustains them through difficult upheavals in their life and provides a sense that whatever the outcome, God will take care of them. We have learned that, in addition to unwavering faith, one should strive to always see the glass as half full rather than half empty.

❖ Research shows that listening to music helps lower blood pressure. One recent study in Finland indicated that stroke victims who listened to music at least one hour daily improved their cognitive and verbal skills more than participants listening to audio books. One of our male clients of 90-plus years attributes his longevity to a passion for the music of the Big Band era—Tommy Dorsey, Harry James and Duke Ellington!

❖ Say yes to a glass of wine or occasional beer, but NO smoking!

❖ Laughter—laugh often and laugh hard. Find humor in everyday life and release those endorphins! Act goofy with your grandchildren, go out with a group of friends and behave like a kid again! Studies have proven that laughter lowers blood pressure, reduces stress and even improves the immune system.

❖ Keep your mind active and your memory sharp. Clients who pursue new hobbies in retirement or enjoy the challenge of crossword puzzles, keep their brain active. They do not think in terms of age or growing old. In their head they remain young and curious. And if you always wanted to learn to knit, write a book (me) or, play a musical instrument (new research indicates that knowing how to read and play music can cause the brain to grow), or even fly a plane—let today be the day you begin. Savor the moments! This is an expression that originates from jazz improvisation—great music that was played but went unrecorded. There is no denying that aging is a challenge, but those individuals who are able to adapt to change, fare much better. We see octogenarians on computers, surfing the internet. Many stay connected with cell phones, IPODS or similar MP3 devices. They are familiar with and use credit cards more than debit cards. These individuals embrace aging and accept the challenges of growing old in a changing world.

❖ Pets provide comfort, contentment and companionship. Studies report that the simple act of petting a dog releases the hormone, oxytocin, which in turn lowers blood pressure and helps decrease anxiety. A purring cat snuggled in a lap, a dog licking a face or reaching a paw out in play—having a pet to care for encourages responsibility, a sense that one is still useful and needed. Realizing the benefits these pets provide, more senior housing complexes now allow residents to have cats, dogs and song birds.

❖ Have a fruit smoothie every morning—the following recipe was shared by Dorothy Smith octogenarian, still curious, still learning, still

playing:
    In blender: 1 banana; 4-5 strawberries;
    4-5 frozen peach slices
    1-2 Tbls. plain yogurt; enough milk to liquefy
    Blend until smooth consistency; makes 2 glasses
    *if using fresh fruit, add 2-3 ice cubes

*"We don't stop playing because we grow old,
    we grow old because we stop playing"*
                                    —George Bernard Shaw

"Will you still need me, will you still feed me,
When I'm sixty-four?"
—Lyrics written by Paul McCartney

CHAPTER TWENTY
Aging Boomers: So Soon?

In 1967, the year that Paul McCartney's song, *When I'm 64,* hit the charts, life expectancy for males was 66.6 years and for females it was 73.1 years. He was 24 years old then but only 16 when he wrote the lyrics. Little did he know that by the time he turned 64 years old in 2006, that it would no longer be considered *old.* This is the same year that the first Baby Boomers began turning 60. When questioned on this milestone birthday, the majority responded first in surprise about how fast the years had passed, and second that they did not *feel old.* This is the group that became teenagers and young adults during the 1960s - a decade that began with the assassination of our President, John F. Kennedy, in 1963 and came to a close in 1969 with headlines that read: *Man Lands On The Moon!* In between was a mixture of love and hate! The Summer of Love, in 1967, brought an estimated 100,000 young people together in the Haight-Ashbury section of San Francisco; while the same year saw anti-war protests all across America in opposition to our being in Vietnam. This band of youth brought with them revolutionary ideas and a call for change in America. No longer content to mirror their parents conservative lifestyle, it is not surprising that they would want to change how growing old in this country is perceived.

The baby boomer generation is the nearly seventy-nine million Americans born between the years 1946-1964. Because of their size and clout, they have had the greatest impact on our society. No intentions of growing old in a rocking chair, they will revamp how elderly are treated in this country. This generation will continue to work, remain active in their community and not entertain any thoughts of entering old age homes. In fact, they have already rejected the traditional nursing home model and even the more recent assisted living facility, which most view as an upscale form of institutional living. In an institutional environment, individuality is lost to the flow of regimented living. There is no time and not enough staff, in most instances, for close bonds to be formed. And there is no history with the individuals sharing living space. Days and time become blurred as one day flows into the next, with death being the only way out.

The Boomers are opting for alternative type housing, such as co-housing, niche communities and other hybrid housing options allowing them to remain independent while aging in place. Latest research published in the *Archives of Internal Medicine*, indicates that even individuals with chronic disease can live to be 100 years old, providing they receive proper medical treatment for their condition. As Boomers explore future housing options, they will be compelled to factor longevity into consideration when scrutinizing cost. And for those individuals requiring some extra help, they will find that home care service will remain the more cost effective choice. Home care enables individuals to remain in their home and as part of their community, to continue to participate in family gatherings, and most important to have the freedom of making personal choices.

Age engenders wisdom learned through life's lessons. We can age gracefully and be content or become embittered at the limitations the years put upon us. One thing that has not changed since Paul McCartney recorded his lyrics in 1967 is the need for human contact, love and friendship.

"Never doubt that a small group of thoughtful committed individuals can change the world, indeed it's the only thing that ever has."

—*Margaret Mead*

CHAPTER TWENTY-ONE
Remnants of Woodstock

Knee and hip replacement surgeries are on the rise predominately because of the baby boom generation. As this generation ages, they are not going to change their lifestyle and become sedentary because of deteriorating joints. A majority of the knee problems involve meniscal and ligament tears due to athletic pursuits. There are in excess of one half million knee replacements and a quarter million hip replacements performed each year, primarily due to wear and tear coupled with osteoarthritis. Living longer means using our joints longer. Unfortunately, these connective tissues are not as durable. Replacements, however, are well-made today, and meant to last.

Cathy was one of the first Baby Boomer generation (1946-1964) clients to contact our agency seeking home care assistance. She was 60 years old and recuperating from a knee replacement. Cathy joked, "I believe the destruction of my knees began in mud, plodding through miles of the rain soaked dirt going to the Woodstock Festival."

It was August, 1969 and Cathy had just graduated from

high school in June. She, like most teenagers during the tumultuous sixties, was part of the love, peace and groovy culture which had a way of 'grabbing hold' of you even if you didn't consider yourself a tie-dyed hippie. And Cathy was far from being a hippie! She grew up in a strict two-parent family where she and her younger sister were doted on by a stay-at-home mom. But change came even to Cathy's rural community. Teenagers in Cathy's high school began dressing Bohemian style, smoking marijuana, listening to Jimi Hendrix and Janis Joplin music on their transistor radios. When many of the girls began wearing long flowing skirts, Cathy felt as though she *almost* fit in, for her mother had always made her wear long skirts, albeit straight and drably. And she had always enjoyed writing poems and music. So it was not that difficult for a couple of her closest friends to talk Cathy into going to Woodstock. Being separated at summer's end, off to different colleges, this was to be their "going away" party!

What Cathy encountered was well beyond anyone's expectation, especially the planners of this concert at Max Yager's Dairy Farm in Bethel, N.Y. What was supposed to be a concert for *some* kids, morphed into a record number 500,000 teenagers and young adults gathering for three days. Needless to say, there were shortages of food, water, porta-toilets, and first aid tents. Torrential downpours flooded the area. Cathy and her friends had to walk in the rain and the mud several miles from where they parked the car. Trudging through that mud has remained a vivid memory for Cathy.

Following college graduation, Cathy moved to a Boston suburb and worked at a private secondary school. She also began a rigorous exercise routine that continued for many years until her knees became excruciatingly painful. Her only option was knee replacement surgery. Having become a grandmother recently, she wanted to enjoy fun outings with her grandson without being in constant pain and discomfort.

Cathy's knee replacement surgery went well. However, because neither family nor friends were readily available to help with post-operative care, she was concerned about her ability to manage on her own. Cathy found out about home care service from her physical therapist at the hospital. She placed a call to our agency and arranged service to start upon hospital discharge. Cathy was like so many others we speak with who are hearing about home care for the first time, and also learning that service can be tailored to each individual's need, lasting as long or short a period of time as wanted.

Cathy's initial care plan required assistance with personal care and ambulation. Pain limited mobility. She also had to protect herself against falls. We set Cathy's service up for two hours, five days with Lee Ann, one of our aides. Lee Ann started each day by helping Cathy with personal care. The aide also prepared well-balanced, high fiber meals and made sure Cathy drank lots of fluids in order to prevent constipation, and bladder infections. Although Cathy was receiving physical therapy on an out - patient basis, Lee Ann needed to help Cathy with range of motion exercises and ambulation at home. The purpose here was to avoid stiffness, and to guard against skin breakdown from remaining sedentary too long.

After a few weeks, because Cathy felt so much better, we decreased service to three days, then two. Lee Ann prepared advance meals, such as soups or casseroles, so that Cathy always had a healthy option on the days she was alone. When Cathy felt ready to resume daily living tasks on her own, she terminated home care service altogether. To the best of our knowledge, Cathy is chasing after her toddler grandson and sharing her Woodstock stories.

Life is not measured by the number of breaths we take,
but by the number of moments that take our breath away.

—anonymous

CHAPTER TWENTY-TWO
Woman's Best Friend

Ask any senior where they want to live out their final years and the answer will invariably be "in my own home," However, most individuals seldom consider the viable option of aging in place when they purchase or renovate their home. More often than not, a medical crisis facilitates the discussion.

Among older adults, a fall is the leading cause of injury with death resulting. Statistics indicate that falls with nonfatal injuries also account for the highest number of hospital admissions for this age group. After a fall, an older person frequently becomes fearful of falling again. They begin curtailing social engagements and physical activities. The sedentary lifestyle ultimately fosters a decline in overall health and well-being.

Janet contacted our agency for home care service after returning home from the hospital in a leg cast. Using a step stool to hang drapes, she lost her balance and fell, resulting in a broken leg. Arriving home with crutches and a cast,

Janet was faced with the daunting task of negotiating her front steps. Once indoors, Janet wondered how she would get to bed on the second floor, bathe in a combined tub/shower, and what she would do for clean clothes with a laundry room situated in the basement. Equally troubling, Janet worried if her dog, Jasper— the two had become inseparable—could remain at home.

When Janet's husband died suddenly two years earlier, she was grief-stricken. Having shared forty-three, love-filled years together, life without him seemed impossible. Therefore, when Janet made two major decisions—to sell her home and to adopt a puppy—no one was more shocked than she.

To help ease Janet's grief, a friend, who coincidentally happened to be a dog breeder, offered her a puppy from a recent litter. Initially, Janet was hesitant but one look into the pooch's large brown eyes, the feel of his wet nose under her chin and his musky newborn smell convinced her to adopt the eight-week-old puppy. Her children frowned upon the decision, feeling that the time demanded to housebreak and train the rambunctious pup was too exhausting. Janet felt the opposite. The puppy, named Jasper, pulled her out of the grief that had taken hold of her, giving renewed purpose to the widow's life.

Janet's second major decision to sell her oversized, four-bedroom colonial home happened by chance. Always a beach lover, a cottage in the ocean-side community where the family summered each year suddenly went up for sale. Knowing the smaller, two-level home would be more manageable, Janet immediately put down a deposit. Three

never minded the dog's presence. Oftentimes, she would open the back door to let Jasper into the fenced back yard. Jasper always became excited upon Addie's arrival, fetching toys to attract her attention. But as soon as Addie began her work with Janet, the dog settled down on his cushioned bed and napped. His eyes opened occasionally to check on them and, content that all was well, resumed napping. Addie returned for an hour each evening to help with the meal, clean up the kitchen afterwards, then assist Janet for bed. Before leaving, Jasper always gave Addie a 'doggie kiss' good-night.

After much thought and discussion with her children, Janet decided to keep her home near the ocean and make some first floor modifications. She intended to interview contractors for a new master bedroom with adjoining bath.

The home care service continued until Janet's cast was removed. Janet gradually resumed her former daily routine. As the client took on more of the daily living tasks, Addie's time was decreased. When the day came for Janet to terminate her service with us, she became emotional. It was difficult for her to say good-bye to Addie. Janet was thoroughly appreciative of the help she received enabling her to stay home, but even more so was grateful that her loving and faithful companion, Jasper, was by her side throughout the healing process.

*With the new millennium and the graying of
America we are beginning to service clients
from the Baby Boom generation. They do not
have geriatric related illnesses. They come
onto home care as disabled younger clients
who have been forced into pre-mature
retirement due to Fibromyalgia, Epstein
Barre, Lupus, Lyme Disease and other
'twenty-first century ailments.' These
individuals do not require a nursing home or
rehab center—they are too young; and, most
do not have the financial means to consider an
Assisted Living Facility. They are perfect
candidates for home care, but many know
nothing about this service.*

CHAPTER TWENTY-THREE
If Left Untreated

Lyme Disease is caused by a bacteria which is transmitted to humans by certain species of ticks. Here in the Northeast, it is the deer tick. Lyme Disease was first recognized in the early 1970s when a cluster of children in Old Lyme, CT were initially thought to suffer from juvenile rheumatoid arthritis. The first sign of infection is a circular rash in which the center looks like a bull's eye. Lyme Disease can affect every tissue and major organ in the body. Symptoms include fatigue, chills, fever, headache, muscle and joint pain and swollen lymph nodes. About sixty percent of individuals who do not receive treatment for Lyme's will experience bouts of arthritis along with severe joint pain and swelling. Up to five percent will have chronic neurological complaints for months and years following infection. These include numbness or tingling in hands and feet, problems with concentration and short term memory.

A woman in her late 50s, Jillian came to our service as an embittered, resistant client who had been through a medical nightmare. Marrying her high school sweetheart while still in college, she graduated with a degree in special education. Because she was already pregnant with their first child, Jillian never entered the job market. Her husband was at the beginning of a very successful career in the corporate world and Jillian was delighted to become a stay-at-home mom, just as her mother had been. In no time at all, she became a busy mother with four children and a household to manage. Jillian knew the day would come when she would become an empty nester, but then she and her husband could travel and enjoy their golden years together.

Jillian's health problems emerged when her youngest daughter entered college. Constantly fatigued, she suffered severe headaches, either upon waking or by mid-day. Initially, Jillian thought it was menopause related and sought treatment from her gynecologist. Her symptoms, which included shooting pains, joint swelling, numbness of hands and feet, and problems with concentration worsened. Constant pain ultimately left Jillian severely depressed. Her primary doctor prescribed an anti-depressant and advised counseling.

Jillian thought her life could not get any worse until her husband came home from work one day and asked for a divorce. He felt that Jillian was depressed because her children were grown. If she had a job, his wife would not have the time to wallow in self-pity, seeking attention with "imagined ailments." He also did not want to be burdened with a disabled spouse. Jillian was devastated. "I was as broken as this Christmas ornament I once had—a beautiful glass angel with golden halo that shimmered next to the tree lights. It fell more than once; and each time I glued the broken parts back together—first a fractured wing, then a split halo. But soon it no longer sparkled when hung on the tree because of all the cracks! That's how I felt. Never to be completely whole again!"

Jillian was forced to sell her home as part of the divorce settlement, and downsized to a condominium located near her oldest son, Mike, and his family. Now her primary caregiver, Mike contacted our agency after a chance meeting with Donna, one of our aides, at his mother's condo complex. Donna was providing home care service to another resident when she met Mike in the laundry room, doing his mother's clothes. She sensed immediately that he was stressed out between work, family, and his mother's care. He knew nothing about in-home services, so Donna told him about her work and suggested that he call our agency to inquire about home care for his mother. Mike called the very next morning, with a multitude of questions. He soon realized that home care would benefit both himself and his mother, and contracted for service.

We scheduled Donna to assist Jillian the same days she was at the condo complex with her other client. By this time, Jillian was seeing a mental health counselor. She rarely went anywhere and most days was too tired or in pain to even shower or dress. Jillian's resistance to outside assistance was no surprise. For all the medical professionals seen and money spent, she had no definitive diagnosis or relief. Jillian was at the point of giving up when Donna came into her life.

Donna worked for our agency over fourteen years. Soft-spoken, extremely observant and a good listener, she proved the perfect match for Jillian. When an aide provides a shower, hair shampoo, assists with dressing, and takes care of all the other daily living tasks in a home, a unique bond is inevitable. Donna could see that Jillian was in considerable pain, because it was so difficult for her to just step into the shower. The aide also realized that Jillian's memory lapses were not imagined, having witnessed her struggle with a shopping list, trying to remember a few needed groceries. Frequently her son would have to return for some forgotten items. Donna shared her observations with Jillian's family and our agency nurse.

After watching a TV documentary about Lyme Disease, Mike realized his mother displayed similar symptoms. He immediately scheduled Jillian for blood tests to determine if she had Lyme's Disease. Once Jillian was diagnosed with the illness, she began a treatment regimen. Jillian was initially shocked then relieved to learn that she had an *actual* disease which could be treated. However, she will never be totally pain-free. Apparently, Jillian had been bitten by a deer tick before Lyme Disease was discovered. Once she and her family began to learn more about Lyme's, her daughters recalled that years before, after chaperoning a girl scout hiking trip, their mother developed a mysterious round rash on the outside of one of her legs. She also experienced severe joint pain, which came on suddenly. Her primary care physician attributed the pain to a jazzercise class she was taking. Jillian was told to stop the strenuous exercise routine and let her body heal. Both the rash and her 'exercise injury' soon disappeared and were forgotten. Her Lyme Disease went untreated, and resulted in bouts of inflammatory arthritis with severe joint pain and swelling. Unfortunately, Jillian also was one of the five percent of individuals to develop chronic neurological problems.

Today, Jillian is a different person. She is almost symptom-free, with the exception of occasional joint pain. Once resistant to receiving home care service, she now refuses to go without. Donna continues to grocery shop and do laundry, relieving Mike of the responsibility. He now visits Jillian without having to worry about care giving, and is delighted, as is the rest of her family, to have their mother back!

*Hope is like a road in the country; there was
never a road, but when
many people walk on it, the road comes into
existence*

—Lin Yutang

CHAPTER TWENTY-FOUR
Battle Against Self

Lucy Vodden made headlines twice in 2009. First when it was revealed that John Lennon wrote the song "Lucy In The Sky With Diamonds" based on a picture that his son, Julian, drew of Lucy when the two were four-year-old schoolmates. The second was her obituary. Lucy died at age forty-six after a long battle with Lupus.

Lupus affects approximately 1.5 million Americans. It is an auto-immune disorder that is unpredictable as well as disabling. Symptoms include chronic pain and fatigue. Patients with Lupus are restricted and limited because they tire easily. Individuals with Lupus often do not act or appear sick, and therefore others assume that they are physically fine. This is the unpredictable part of Lupus. Symptoms can be managed with medications, but tragically medical science is yet to discover a cure.

Meg's daughter Stacy noticed our agency ad in her local newspaper and called to inquire about service for her mother. Meg had been living with Lupus for several years. Now in her fifties and going through menopause, hormonal changes exacerbated the disease. Also, her son had recently married and Meg helped plan the splendid outdoor garden wedding. Long periods in the sun coupled with the stress and strain, aggravated Meg's Lupus. She became very ill after the wedding, prompting Stacy to call our agency. Knowing very little about home care, Meg's daughter was specifically concerned about how we matched caregiver and client. She informed us that Meg would likely make light of needing home care assistance, particularly personal care.

After describing the duties of both homemaker and aide, and explaining our matching process, it was determined that homemaker service would be best for her mother.

A service plan was designed to send a homemaker twice weekly for three hours each day. Stacy agreed that it was best to arrange the service at the beginning and end of the week.   Laundry would be done on Tuesday; grocery shopping and necessary errands were scheduled on Friday. Our biggest challenge was convincing Meg to accept help! From our first phone call, she was resistant. A subsequent visit to the home with Stacy present was met with equal resistance but confirmed what Stacy had told us about her mother. Meg appeared exhausted and in chronic pain. She could barely sit and focus on the conversation. Ultimately, Stacy convinced her mother to give home care service a chance. What finally prompted Meg to say okay, was the assurance from us that the service could be put in place on a short-term basis, and the time would be adjusted to meet *her* needs. Also, once she was feeling better and able to resume her household duties, we would terminate the service.

We matched Meg with Jennifer, a homemaker employed at our agency for over ten years. She is very task-oriented and knows how to respect a client's privacy. The majority of the clients we provide service to are elderly and homebound. Many are lonely and benefit greatly from socialization. Therefore, our aides and homemakers will readily chat with them while cleaning, folding laundry, or preparing a meal. However, Meg was neither elderly nor homebound. Because of her Lupus flair-up she needed to rest and limit all activities, not chat or hover while Jennifer was working.

Jennifer was an ideal match for Meg. She accustomed herself to Meg's household routine and food preferences quickly, and got her work done without requiring Meg's input. Jennifer always had a hot, nutritious breakfast waiting when Meg was finished with her personal care. She would then set to work on the homemaker tasks. After a couple of weeks, Meg confided to Stacy how pleased she was with Jennifer, and wished she had known about home care service much sooner. Stacy was delighted that her mother was sleeping later in the morning and taking afternoon naps instead of doing tiring housework, laundry and grocery shopping. Meg also was eating home-cooked, nutritious meals rather than the frozen foods she routinely micro-waved, when too weary to cook conventional meals. After a few weeks, Meg looked and felt much stronger. When she decided the home care service was no longer needed, Meg called our agency to terminate. She thanked us for sending Jennifer and informed us, "Anytime I need service again, I definitely want Jennifer!"

Strength does not come
from physical capacity.
It comes from an
indomitable will.
　　　　　—Mohandas K. Gandhi

CHAPTER TWENTY-FIVE
Not Always What Appears To Be

The client was reluctant to share much information on the phone, preferring instead, a face-to-face home visit. Her name was Cara-Lee. A woman in her early 60s, she recently recovered from a three-week bout with the flu. Having low energy after the flu is common, but for someone with Fibromyalgia, the fatigue can be overwhelming. Cara-Lee had been living with Fibromyalgia for over ten years. She understood how to pace herself. However, a series of stressful events during the fall and winter months had weakened her immune system, causing a medical crisis.

Our agency nurse was welcomed by Cara-Lee, a tall attractive woman with graying hair, upon arriving at the duplex building located in a secluded part of an upscale neighborhood. She was escorted into the living room which was tastefully decorated in French Provincial style. On the mantel sat three long-necked apothecary jars, each containing colorful mini-candies. "High energy runs in my family! My mother, in her mid- 80s, is up at the crack of dawn to wash clothes and hang them outside to dry," Cara-Lee said, easing into conversation. Once high energy like her parents and siblings, she was faced with the reality of toning down her fast-paced lifestyle. She went on to explain that individuals with Fibromyalgia may not look sick, but the pain they suffer is real and debilitating.

Cara-Lee graduated college with high honors. Following graduation, she was hired by a large ad agency in Boston, where she met and married her now ex-husband. Cara-Lee described the marriage as brief and volatile. Married less than two years, they had moved a half-dozen times. Following the divorce, she moved back home with her parents. Determined to rebuild her life as quickly as possible, Cara-Lee immediately found a job and relocated to her current duplex. She also began volunteering at the local library and joined a book club. Over the next few years, work, friends and family kept Cara-Lee extremely active.

Fibromyalgia symptoms began in her late 40s. She would wake up stiff and in pain. Some days Cara-Lee dreaded going to work, knowing that she would be exhausted and overwhelmed by the pain before the day was half over. Most nights she tossed and turned, finding it difficult to sleep due to the discomfort.

Fibromyalgia is a chronic pain syndrome that affects more women than men. The cause, which is unknown may be genetic. There is no cure. The standard method of diagnosing the syndrome is with a tender-point exam. This consists of a practitioner pressing on approximately eighteen different parts of the body to check for muscle discomfort. Once diagnosed, physical therapy is usually recommended. It is extremely important to discover what works in terms of pain relief and a good night's sleep. Also, stress must be closely monitored to avoid exacerbating the chronic condition.

Cara-Lee did not get diagnosed quickly. Rather, she went through a series of medical tests and was prescribed anti-depressants. She feared not being able to work and having to rely on disability insurance. Because she did not *appear* ill, her family and friends questioned why a single, middle-aged woman with no major responsibilities, should need to go on disability. They wondered whether her pain was imaginary— a psychological condition—and she needed counseling.

Nearly two years after her symptoms surfaced, Cara-Lee discovered she suffered from Fibromyalgia. Attending a presentation at the library, Cara-Lee listened as the guest speaker described the symptoms and chronic pain associated with the disease, and quickly identified with everything being said.

Once diagnosed, Cara-Lee was relieved to have a name for her condition. She was able to find relief through the combination of an aquatics program at the Y combined with physical therapy. She also learned how to juggle work, home, family and outside interests while keeping stress and multi-tasking at manageable levels. However, a succession of unforeseen events beginning in early September and continuing well into the winter months proved too overwhelming for Cara-Lee. Her older brother and sister retired to Florida as soon as they were eligible for pensions. When her father became ill shortly after Labor Day, he relied on Cara-Lee for rides to medical appointments. Because her mother no longer drove, both parents depended on Cara-Lee for their grocery shopping and errands. In November her father passed away, leaving her elderly mother to rely solely on Cara-Lee.

Overwhelmed with the additional responsibilities, Cara-Lee's immune system weakened and she became severely ill with the flu. While sick, her Fibromyalgia intensified to the point of non-stop pain and sleepless nights. In addition to stressing over her messy home and piled-up laundry, Cara-Lee also worried about her mother's needs.

Cara-Lee heard about our agency through word-of-mouth. Someone in her book club was friendly with a neighbor who used our services. However, Cara-Lee was leery about allowing a stranger into her home, but following our nurse's initial visit she felt reassured and eager for help to begin.

Our care plan emphasized short-term, homemaker service. Cara-Lee was matched with Rose, an older woman who appeared fine on the 'outside', but suffered a deep sadness within. She carried the grief of losing her only son, killed in a car accident while serving in the military. Initially, Rose was filled with rage questioning why, if her son had to die, couldn't it have been as a hero for his country rather than in a senseless mangle of steel. Rose realized, however, that over time her rage would become corrosive and debilitating. Instead, she chose to become a caregiver, reaching out to assist others in need. Her kind, gentle manner immediately put Cara-Lee at ease. Rose provided assistance with laundry, grocery shopping and housework two hours twice weekly.

After six weeks Cara-Lee's house was back to a manageable state. During that time, she rested and kept stress at bay. Once her Fibromyalgia symptoms were back under control and her energy levels replenished, Cara-Lee no longer needed Rose's help. Feeling extremely satisfied with the service received, she decided to contract homemaker service for her mother. Having an agency employee do her mother's grocery shopping and errands was one less responsibility for Cara-Lee to worry about, thereby minimizing stress, with the added benefit of affording Cara-Lee more quality time with her mother.

Give us O Lord grateful hearts which do
not waste time complaining
                                    —St. Thomas Aquinas

CHAPTER TWENTY-SIX
A Simple Thanks

The card came as a pleasant surprise because we had only serviced the client five months. His daughter wrote a note of appreciation, expressing how grateful she was for the service that allowed her father to die at home with dignity.

Because most of our work is done via the telephone, rarely is there face-to-face contact, and therefore the role our office staff undertakes providing a quality service to clients often goes unrecognized. With each new intake, voices on the end of a phone line immediately go to work fulfilling our mission statement - *enable an individual to remain living independently, and with dignity, at home and in their community.* This concept guarantees that everyone possesses the right to remain at home within familiar surroundings and that we, as home care professionals, have the ability to make it happen!

Following a medical crisis, in order for an individual to return home from a hospital or rehab facility, they need an agency to begin service within twenty-four to forty-eight hours. With this consideration in mind, we at Ideal *only* accept cases that we can readily service. Few people appreciate the meticulous attention to detail required to set up home care service for each client. A two-hour-weekly case may entail every bit as much planning—paperwork, phone calls, faxes and scheduling—as a seven-day, split-shift case. The process requires keen listening skills - the ability to hear in another's voice the sound of panic, fear, hesitation, confusion, and resistance. Genuine, heartfelt concern for each client oftentimes extends to immediate family. We come to know each person as though they were family because we share their life story, which unfolds over time: a sound of joy at the birth of a great grandchild; the tears of sorrow with the death of a spouse; relief when the doctor gives good news; everyone celebrating when the client, who has had multiple medical crisis, hits the one-hundred-year milestone!

A personal note of gratitude is always emotionally touching, as well as acknowledgement of a job well done. But there is no less accountability on the part of office staff to the client who does not share sentiments of gratitude. Our commitment that individuals have the right to remain living at home independently and with dignity versus institutionalization extends to all our clients.

Home care not only allows an individual to remain within familiar surroundings, but also relieves family of added demands, thus providing for quality time together. Recognizing that in-home care should always be viewed as an option when one requires assistance with daily living tasks, our office staff compiled the following list of frequently asked questions as a useful guide when considering home care service.

FREQUENTLY ASKED QUESTIONS

How much will home care service cost and how do I pay?

Answer: Service is generally contracted on an hourly basis and varies from agency to agency. A Metlife Mature Market Institute 2011 survey lists national average rates for home health aides at $21.00/hour and homemaker rates at $19.00/hour. Agencies generally require that employees submit signed invoices from their clients on a weekly or bi-weekly basis, and, in turn, bill clients from these pay slips. Clients should always be given a copy of signed invoices so they can accurately cross reference hours received with hours billed.

What happens if my aide/homemaker cannot come?

Answer: Home care agencies frequently maintain lists of aides who are available on short notice to fill in when a co-worker calls out sick. Even if the employee contacts the agency after hours or over the weekend, the 'on-call' supervisor may still be able to locate a replacement from a list of employees.

Can my aide/homemaker drive me to appointments if a family member cancels at the last minute and I need transportation?

Answer: This issue is a bit complicated and the answer may ultimately depend on several variables. Because transportation takes place off premises, it is not routinely covered under home care services and represents legal risk to the agency. On the other hand, a client or family member could conceivably sign a waiver absolving the agency and employee of any liability in the event of an accident. As a rule of thumb, most reputable home care agencies tend to err on the side of caution and refuse to provide transportation.

If a client has an emergency after hours and will not be home when their homemaker/aide comes, how do they cancel this service?

Answer: It is not uncommon for home care agencies to maintain 24/7, emergency answering services and are able to relay messages to staff when a client needs to cancel service on short notice.

If a client is being discharged from the hospital or nursing home how do they begin new service or restart their suspended service?

Answer: When a client is released from a hospital or rehab center and needs to reinstate services on short notice, most agencies possess a protocol to ensure continuity of care. In the event that the call to resume service is placed after normal business hours, the 'on call' coordinator will telephone the aide or homemaker and handle the formal paperwork once back in the office.

If a homemaker/aide arrives to a client's home and they cannot gain access, what will they do?

Answer: A common sense approach usually works best when unable to gain access to a client's home. The worker may knock at the door for a prolonged period. If a rear entrance or ground floor windows are available, they will try to gain access or attract the client's attention. The agency coordinator may phone the client or emergency contact to determine if there has been an unreported medical emergency and the client is hospitalized. Sometimes other social service professionals such as the visiting nurses, meals-on-wheels, physical therapist, etc. may be able to shed light on the client's whereabouts. As a last resort, the police may need to be contacted. This is done as a precautionary measure in the event that, critically ill, the client is unable to come to the door and requires medical assistance.

If there is a change in client condition or any concerns, how are they addressed?

Answer: The nature and severity of any change in a client's condition must be assessed by proper medical authority. Frequently a home care agency will contact family to inform them of changes in a loved one's physical well being. Ultimately family members will decide what is in the client's best interest.

Those who danced were thought to be quite
insane by those who could not hear the music
                                    —Angela Monet

CHAPTER TWENTY-SEVEN
Less Is More

Ideal Home Care recently celebrated thirty years in business. We have been through periods of growth and prosperity as well as the more recent economic downturn. Over the years, colleagues occasionally asked why our agency never joined a national franchise or added a skilled nursing component to our job description. The potential for growth and profit would have increased. Instead, we chose to remain a small, family-owned home care agency with a main office in Rhode Island and satellite branch in neighboring Massachusetts. At one time we began the Medicare certification process. But after discussing with our staff what lay ahead if we proceeded, the decision to remain small was unanimous. Our motto became—"we do one thing and we do it well!"

Most of our clients experience chronic disabilities. They are routinely maintained in the home setting at an affordable cost which is far less expensive than placement in a nursing home or assisted living facility, providing round-the-clock care. And for those home care clients that require seven-day service, the cost is usually flat-rated. For example, our agency switches from an hourly rate to an economical, flat rate for private clients receiving more than 20 hours per week or 30 hours per month. The 2011 national average daily rate of $21.00/hour for a home health aide and $19.00/hour for a homemaker has remained unchanged since 2010. However, results of the same Met Life 2011 survey of long term care costs show increases in nursing home ($239.00/day for a private room), assisted living ($3,477/month, and adult day care ($70.00/day). As costs for custodial care mushroom from year to year, the economics of home care remain relatively stable and unchanged.

In 1982 Ideal Home Care competed with less than two dozen agencies for the Rhode Island private market. Today, there are at least three times that number of agencies. Our state is not alone. With the graying of America, there has been an influx of home care agencies, predominately independently owned franchises, sprouting up across the country. Quality, type of service, costs and level of commitment vary dramatically from agency to agency. The administrator overseeing an agency sets the tone in terms of overall values and delivery of service.

The Olmstead Act grants Americans the constitutional right to receive care at home and reside in a community setting. And yet, putting a home care plan in place for a loved one is not an easy task. Families must be pro-active about keeping their loved ones at home and understand what kind of care is both needed and affordable. AARP's *Caregiving Resource Center* website is a good place to begin an agency search. They have a Care Provider Locater link where users enter a zip code and local agencies plus costs pop up.

Just as one would research a nursing home or other residential facility before contracting for service, the same diligence must be exercised with home care. Organizations such as Press Ganey monitor patient satisfaction in hospitals, nursing homes, rehab facilities and home care agencies while working to improve both health care standards and performance. Rhode Island Department of Health, our licensing agency, contracts with Press Ganey and publishes the results on their website.

Health care, especially where the elderly consumer is concerned, contains many hidden costs that can wreck havoc with a seemingly sensible budget. Rates quoted residents entering an assisted living facility are frequently nothing more than *base estimates.* Every service that falls outside the facility's essential package incurs additional expense. For example, when a forgetful client needs to be given his pills by a med tech, there may be a surcharge, the fee determined by the number of separate medications. The resident requires assistance with laundry, grooming, transportation, special diet, etc.—each item incurs additional expense—an outlay of money that was never factored into the original decision to opt for institutional care. Taking this to the extreme, an elderly client may be compelled to pay for something as innocuous as a light bulb if it is determined that the damaged bulb came from a bedside lamp rather than one of the facilities lighting units!

As we move from servicing the Greatest Generation to the Baby Boomer Generation, the need for home care services will increase. The delivery model will adjust as this generation demands to 'age in place' and because home care is still less costly than institutionalization. Now if only our government and state officials could do the math and figure out what economists have been saying about home care for years.

Old age is the most unexpected of
all the things that happen to a man
                              —Leon Trotsky

CHAPTER TWENTY-EIGHT
What Next?

As an administrator in home care for thirty years and baby boomer approaching retirement, a frequent topic of discussion with peers is how I see the future for aging in this country. Looking back over the last three decades lends a more accurate assessment of what lies ahead.

The elderly population has always been our primary market. In April, 1982 when we opened our home care agency, the typical client was born in the late 1800s to early 1900s. They lived longer than their parents whose average life span was less than 60 years. This group of seniors grew up in an America with more farms than factories and where kids worked six or seven days a week, sometimes up to twelve hours a day. They were alive in 1911 when the Triangle Shirtwaist Fire, one of the deadliest tragedies in our history, occurred in New York City. What followed was legislation improving safety standards in factories, better working conditions, and new laws governing child labor. This is the generation that shared family time around the dinner table and conversation on the front porch. Church was always a part of their life. As teenagers, if their parents owned a Victor Talking Machine, they listened to the Italian tenor, Enrico Caruso. They owned hand-cranked Model T cars, shopped the Sears Roebuck catalog, and used installment plans for major purchases only. Anything else they needed was bought with cash from savings.

The generation we currently serve is known as *The Greatest Generation,* (born 1914-1924) and those born at the beginning of The Great Depression (1929-1939). These individuals lived through, and many fought in World War II. After the war and anxious to get on with life, they moved to suburbs in record numbers and began raising families. The men used their GI bill for college education. Women who replaced the male worker during the war (given the moniker *Rosie the Riveter)* returned to their role as homemakers, albeit now in suburbia. This group of seniors lived in communities where they knew their neighbors and readily relied on each other for help. Families spent quality time playing games such as *Scrabble*, and putting together jigsaw puzzles. Rather than a multitude of specialists, they had only one health provider, the family doctor, who made house calls. A link between cancer and smoking had not been discovered yet. Most males already smoked, and now women of this generation took up the habit in great numbers, continuing into old age with emphysema and portable oxygen tank in tow. Having grown up during the Great Depression, most remain frugal to this day, seeking out bargains when they shop and carrying minimal debt.

Technology represents another major change for this generation, who had no computers, faxes or cell phones. A huge timesaver for them was the typewriter. Today, we have instantaneous access to information through cyberspace and the world moves at a much quicker pace. Mahatma Gandhi said "there is more to life than increasing its speed." Trying to keep pace with machines does not interest this group of seniors. Theirs is still a slower, simpler way of life, which translates into face-to-face contact, phone conversations on their land line and correspondence by snail mail.

Many of our female clients never worked outside their home following marriage, and as their own parents approached end of life, these woman provided care for them at home. A difficult concept for this group of seniors to grasp is that they now have daughters and granddaughters with careers demanding long hours at work and less time at home with family. Over the last thirty years, as more women entered the job market, we at Ideal Home Care have documented an increased need for long term care with this senior population.

The over-65-year-old segment in this country has grown to forty million. As the baby boom generation (those born 1946-1964) continues to shift into retirement years, these numbers are projected to hit fifty-five million by 2020. This seismic change will catapult the demand for long term care in this country to an all-time high. Known as the generation that refuses to grow old, essayist Tom Wolfe says in Tom Brokaw's book *Boom, Voices of the Sixties,* that boomers "trying to look twenty-seven by dressing like they're thirteen leads to a new aging disease, juvenility, to go with senility." However, those of us who were a product of the tumultuous sixties like to change and restructure to meet our evolving needs. This will translate into an attitude change on aging, accepting the process and viewing it not as a conclusion of one's productive years, but as a lifelong learning experience.

Determined to stay at home, this generation will refuse to consider nursing homes! They built the first "McMansions." outfitting them with the latest gadgets such as home gyms, gourmet kitchens, Jacuzzis and aromatherapy baths. Although now downsizing to smaller living spaces, they have no intention of giving up these amenities. The boomers will not hesitate to spend money for home modifications allowing them to age in place. Architects are currently designing single level, easily accessible homes, with this aging group in mind. Called universal design, these homes have no stairs to negotiate, affording easy accessibility throughout. Some of their most important features are wider door openings, walk-in showers, door levers instead of knobs (which work well for individuals of all ages-from young fingers learning to open doors to older, arthritic hands). Bathroom shower seats now come in fold-down versions and grab bars blend in as decorative accessories rather than safety equipment. Lighting is sensor or voice controlled; laundry rooms are located off master bedrooms; outdoor areas have no-mow lawns as well as heated driveways to eliminate snow shoveling in colder climates.

Baby boomers are health conscious. They constantly seek out the latest holistic health trends from organic foods to chemical-free environments and are eager to try alternative therapies such as acupuncture, Reiki, as well as New Age therapies. The benefits of exercise will keep them physically fit and living longer which means home care for nonagenarians and centenarians will be a growing need.

Dr. William H. Thomas, a well-known reformer of long term care, calls himself a "nursing home abolitionist." He is the founder of the Green House Project and Eden Alternative which offers a new approach to long term care. Thomas intends to replace nursing homes nationwide with private residences that house eight to ten people. He aims to change the negative view on aging in America, focusing on how much we can learn from our elders.

Assisted living facilities may be a choice for this aging generation, however, they are already too familiar with this type of housing because their parents were the first group to have resided in them. Many will see these facilities for what they are: a fresh coat of paint and bright new shutters in the front, but bare in the back with peeling paint. Savvy consumers will be leery of 'the third floor.' In most assisted living facilities, there is an Alzheimer's unit that is not shown on the marketing tour. The residents from this unit can be a reminder to the more independent individuals of where they actually are—in an institution for the aged, masking as a resort. With interest rates plummeting and investments dwindling, gone are the days when the family homestead could be sold and family inheritance used to finance a move into a luxury facility. There is greater risk today of outliving savings. In some areas this has already happened, resulting in seniors being dropped off at homeless shelters because they have nowhere else to go. This may be one of the reasons why, in recent years, there has been a resurgence of multi-generational living—three or more generations residing in single-family residences—and in add-on suites (also called a granny flat). Combining households as well as financial resources safeguards family assets and enables adult children to closely monitor the changing needs of their aging parents.

A unique multi-generational development, *Treehouse on Home Meadow*, located in Easthampton, Massachusetts, was modeled after a community in central Illinois. Here, seniors live alongside young families raising foster and adopted children. Because elders and those in foster care systems are two groups often shunned by society at large, bringing them together creates a synergistic bond.

Several new housing trends, which encourage seniors to live independently are developing across the country. Elder or senior co-housing consists of individuals residing in communities populated by older adults. Residents assume a proactive role in the design, operation and overall management of their neighborhood. Individuals own their homes, while sharing common facilities. This model encourages interaction with neighbors, such as meals, recreation and exercise, thereby avoiding isolation and loneliness.

For individuals 50 years and older who want to live independently within their community, and have no intention of entering a nursing home or assisted living, organizations are forming that anticipate and address their needs. One such program is Beacon Hill Village in Boston, Massachusetts. For an annual membership fee, this non-profit group provides a wide array of services from in-home care to transportation. Nursing homes can cost up to $12,000/month and assisted living facilities, with all their amenities, add up to even more expense. Places like Beacon Hill Village provide a network of resources that cost considerably less and enable individuals to remain living independently in the familiar comfort of their own home.

Technology will benefit aging boomers who want to remain living independently. Currently gadgets exist to keep one connected with emergency medical personnel, well-checks from a doctor's office, reminders to take medications as well as wireless capability to see and communicate with loved ones, be they near or far away. Already in use by boomers who want to keep watch over an elderly parent living alone, these home monitoring systems are both affordable and easy to use. Technology will only continue to evolve and become more sophisticated, enabling aging boomers to remain living at home within their community.

Transportation remains a critical need for older Americans. For a nominal fee and with advance notice, most communities provide van transport to medical appointments. Some van services include local shopping trips on specific days of the week and for set times. A program implemented in New York City utilizes yellow school buses, that would otherwise remain parked during the day, to transport seniors to the market and shopping centers throughout the city. However, what is lacking is transportation for *spontaneous* events, such as lunch with a friend or a movie matinee. As the boomers continue to age and develop health issues, many will no longer be able to drive or obtain ready access to transportation. Planners need to address this essential issue in order for seniors to remain engaged members of their community.

Much like Wendell Berry's fictionalized agrarian community of Port William, in which residents belong as part of a membership, aging boomers are now beginning to recognize the importance of establishing progressive communities where neighbors befriend one another and help meet common needs. At the risk of becoming an aging society that is isolated and helpless—stripped of our independence and dignity—aging boomers must reconfigure the way we view growing old in America, reform long term care policies and develop new trends which promote aging in place surrounded by all that is familiar.

NOTES

Introduction

11 aarp.org/projected long term care survey, 2007.
13 Starfish Story from *"The Star Thrower"* essay by Loren Eiseley published in *The Unexpected Universe*, California: Harcourt, Brace & World, 1969.

Chapter One - No Expiration Date

15 **"active life was presumably over for them,":** Alice Brown, *Joint Owners in Spain,* short story in her collection of *Meadow Grass, Tales of New England Life.* Published 1896.

15 **"to be in an institution is to be outside the reach"** : Tom Koch, *A Place in Time: Care Givers for Their Elderly.* NY: Praeger Books, 1993.

15 www.iom.edu/reports/2008/aging america

Chapter Two - Cancelled for Lack of Interest
17-19 Course syllabus notes from *Home Care for the Elderly – A Practical Approach to Independent Living:* Anne Rachin, Fall, 1982.
19 *In Those Years.* poem by Adrienne Rich.

19 In 2006 the government expended approximately $7,000: Val J. Halamandares, *Caring Thoughts*. Caring Magazine, September, 2006.

Chapter Three -Parkinson's: Not Part of the Plan

20 **"Life comes down to a series of choices."** : Michael J. Fox, June 29, 2011 excerpt from closing speech of the Society for Human Resource management's 63rd Annual Conference and Exposition.
www.shrm.org/publications/hrnews/pages/foxadvises.

Chapter Six - Red is for the Heart

37 National Wear Red Day campaign.
www.goredforwomen.org.

Chapter Seven - Keeper of My Memories

38 **"You have sweet memories"**: Ken Freeman, *Memories*. Poem reprinted with permission from Fall 2006 *care ADvantage*, a publication of the Alzheimer's Foundation of America.

39 *The 36-Hour Day*, Nancy L. Mace, M.A. and Peter V. Rabins, M.D., M.P.H. Johns Hopkins Press, Baltimore, MD., 1981.

42 *Ma Is Back!*, Brad Pitman with Nancy A. Driscoll. ICAN, Ltd., Attleboro, MA., 2010.

Chapter Twelve - Pushed and Pulled

60 **"Trees grow stronger over the years, rivers wider."** : United Nations Secretary General Kofi Annan, on growing old.

63 average daily rate for nursing home, www.pbn.com/RI-nursing home- assisted living rates

Chapter Thirteen - Lifetime Commitment

66 In 2011 the average national cost for a private nursing home room: www.lifehealthpro.com/2011/10/25/metlife-mmi-survey.

Chapter Fifteen - Death is Not Optional

73 **"The symphony of life should end with a grand finale of peace":** Lin Yutang, *The Importance of Living*, 1937.

74 **"death is only an instant"** : Stephen Kiernen, *Last Rights*. New York: St. Martin's Press, 2006.

Chapter Sixteen - A Full Life

78 occupant odors: www.glamzzle.com/occupant odor

Chapter Eighteen - A Reverence for Nature

84   the yellow rumped warbler: April Pulley Sayre, *Home at Last: A Song of Migration*. New York: Henry Holt and Co., 1998.

Chapter Twenty - Aging Boomers: So Soon?

93 Latest research published in the Archives of Internal Medicine: Lindsey Tanner (AP), *To 100 and beyond*. Attleboro, MA: The Sun Chronicle, 2/12/08.

Chapter Twenty-One - Remnants of Woodstock

96 *www.woodstock.com/themusic.php*

Chapter Twenty-Three - If Left Untreated

104 *www.lymediseaseguide.org/lyme-disease-history*

Chapter Twenty-Four Battle Against Self

109
www.boston.com/bostonglobe/obituaries/articles/2009/09

Chapter Twenty-Seven - Less is More

124 www.metlifematuremarketsurvey

124 www.aarpcaregivingresourceguide

125 www.health.ri.gov/quality reports/ home health agencies

Chapter Twenty-Eight - What's Next?

129 **"there is more to life than increasing its speed"**, Mahatma Gandhi, October 2, 1869 – January 30, 1948. Indian leader.

129 **"trying to look twenty-seven"** : Tom Wolfe, essayist interviewed by Tom Brokaw, *Boom, Voices of the Sixties.* New York: Random House, Inc., 2007.

131 Dr. William Thomas calls himself a "nursing home abolitionist": Mark Abromaitis, *Leading a 'social revolution'.* The Erickson Tribune, May, 2007.

131 Eugene Moore, *Check the third floor*, Attleboro, MA: The Sun Chronicle, 5/14/07.

132 Hoya El Nasser, *Seniors at Home in Co-housing*, USA Today, 5/4/09.

133 A program implemented in New York City utilizes yellow school buses: Blair S. Walker, *Busing Older Adults, New York Style*. AARP Bulletin, October, 2009.

134 Wendell Berry, *A Place on Earth*, Boston, MA: Harcourt, Brace, 1967.

RESOURCE GUIDE

AARP
601 E Street, NW
Washington, DC 20049
888-687-2277
www.aarp.org

Alzheimer's Association National Office
225 N. Michigan Ave., FL. 17
Chicago, IL 60621
24/7 Helpline: 1-800-272-3900
www.alz.org

Alzheimer's Foundation of America
322 8th Ave. 7th FL
New York, NY 10001
866-232-8484
www.alzfdn.org

Alzheimer's Association – RI Chapter
245 Waterman St., Suite 306
Providence, RI 02906
www.alz-ri.org

American Cancer Society
250 Williams Street NW
Atlanta, GA 30303
1-800-227-2345
www.cancer.org

American Diabetes Association
 Center for Information
1701 North Beauregard Street
Alexandria, VA 22311
1-800-342-2383
www.diabetes.org

American Heart Association
7272 Greenville Ave.
Dallas, TX 75231
1-800-AHA-USA-1
1-800-242-8721
www.heart

American Parkinson Disease Association
135 Parkinson Avenue
Staten Island, NY 10305
718-981-8001
800-223-2732
www.apdaparkinson.org

The Amyotrophic Lateral Sclerosis Association, RI Chapter
1637 Warwick Ave.
Warwick, RI 02889
(401) 732-1609
webri.alsa.org

Arthritis Foundation
P.O. Box 7669
Atlanta, GA 30357
800-283-7800
www.arthritis.org

Arthritis Health Center
www.arthritis.webmd.co

Beacon Hill Village
74 Joy Street
Boston, MA
617-723-9713
info@beaconhillvillage.org

Beyond Barriers – barrier free products to improve daily living
conditions
1-800-561-2223
beyondbarriers.com

Eden Alternative
P.O. Box 18369
1900 S. Clinton Avenue
Rochester, NY 14618
585-461-3951

Greenhouse Project
caring homes for meaningful lives
www.thegreenhouseproject.org

Ideal Home Care Service, Inc
8 Martin Avenue
North Providence, RI 02904
401-353-2230
www.idealhomecare.org

www.lotsahelpinghands.com
connecting people through the power
of community

Lyme Disease Association, Inc.
P.O. Box 1438
Jackson, NJ 08527
888-366-6611
www.lymediseaseassociation.org

Marshall Domestics
12 Factory Street
West Warwick, RI
800-556-7440
(health care linens)

National Association of Home Builders
www.nahb.org/universal design

National Association for Home Care & Hospice (NAHC)
228 Seventh Street, SE
Washington, DC 20003
Caring Magazine is published by NAHC
www.caringmagzine.com
202-547-5277

National Eye Institute
31 Center Drive MSC 2510
Bethesda, MD 20892
www.nei.nih.gov

National Fibromyalgia Association
2121 S Towne Centre Suite 300
Anaheim, CA 92806
714-921-0150
fmaware.org

National Lupus Association
2000 L Street, NW Suite 410
Washington, DC 20036
202-349-1155
www.lupus.org

National Multiple Sclerosis Society
733 Third Avenue 3rd FL
NY, NY 10017
1-800-314-4867
www.nationalmssociety.org

National Parkinson Foundation
1501 N.W. 9th Avenue/Bob Hope Road
Miami, FL 33136
1-800-473-4636
www.parkinson.org

Senior Resource
877-793-7901
seniorresource.com

Treehouse at Easthampton Meadow
www.treehousebc.com

U.S. Department of Veterans Affairs
810 Vermont Avenue, NW
Washington, DC 20420
www.va.gov

The following Check List can be used as a basic guide when preparing a home care plan:

Assessment of needs: Personal Care_____ Homemaker _____
Combination of both _____

Arrange for Geriatric Care Specialist to assist with assessment if needed _____

Meals-on-Wheels _____   Lifeline _____

In preparation of home care service:

Products for personal care such as towels, wash cloths, personal items, etc._____
Cleaning products for homemaker_____
Special dietary needs for meal prep _____ (i.e. allergies, diabetic, low salt)
Advance meal prep needs _____
Emergency contact phone #s _____
Medication list in designated place (in the event of emergency transport) _____
Pet immunizations current _____

Determine if durable medical equipment is needed. Most common DME for elderly include:

wheelchair _____ walker _____ cane _____ tub/shower stool _____ raised toilet seat _____ commode _____

washable bed pads for incontinence _____
(cotton is better than plastic pads which tend to slide. Taping in place is not recommended because tape can stick to skin and cause a tear in older, thinner skin.)

Simple home modifications:

Lever door handles _____ removal of scatter rugs, extension cords, & other tripping hazards _____
easy phone access _____ slip-proof bath mat _____
hand-held shower _____ tub/toilet grab bars _____
motion sensor lights _____ (in addition to outdoors, can be used indoors for safety of nighttime trips to the bathroom)
Contact local Council on Aging for community resources such as respite, day care, support groups _____

Transportation needs _____ Outdoor ramp _____

K

kindness, 32, 33
knee, 95, 97

L

laughter, 67, 79, 89
longevity, 87, 89, 93
Lupus, 104, 109, 111, 146

M

Macular Degeneration, 77
Medicaid, 18, 20, 75
Medicare, 18, 20, 74, 75, 123
modifications, 49, 52, 63, 66, 103,
  130, 149
multi-generational, 15, 131, 132
Multiple Sclerosis, 53, 55, 146

N

nature, 54, 84, 86, 122
nutrition, 18, 35, 39, 44, 57, 58, 87,
  88

O

Olmstead Act, 124

osteoarthritis, 85, 95

P

Parkinson's, 21, 22, 23, 24, 136
pet, 90, 102
positive outlook, 81
productive, 84, 130

R

rural, 78, 83, 96

S

Schweitzer, 14
socialization, 45, 81, 111
stress, 58, 89, 110, 114, 115
stroke, 69, 89

T

technology, 20, 74
transportation, 58, 62, 120, 121,
  125, 132, 133
Type A personality, 80

About the Author

Anne R. Rachin has been a home care administrator for the past thirty years, owning Ideal Home Care in North Providence, RI with her husband, Barry. A graduate of the University of Rhode Island with a Bachelor of Arts in Psychology, she counseled in a community clinic and worked with veterans returning home from Vietnam, before finding her niche in the field of Gerontology. She has dedicated her career to assisting individuals in Rhode Island and Southeastern Massachusetts to remain living at home with independence and dignity.

During this time, Anne, her administrative staff and caregivers have participated in community programs such as Make a Difference Day, collecting and shipping emergency supplies in the aftermath of 9/11, and supporting our military troops and their loved ones. The focus has always been the significance of home and family.

Using a percentage of proceeds from this book, Anne's dream is to implement an 'animeals' program for seniors in need of food for their pets. *All That's Familiar* is her first book. Anne resides in Massachusetts with her husband, two daughters and two dogs.

Anne can be reached at www.allthatsfamiliar.com

PUBLISHER'S NOTE

Now that you have finished reading this book, the author would be most grateful if you would take the time to post an honest review of it on Amazon, Barnes & Noble or any other online bookseller's web site.
Anyone with an Amazon account can post reviews, even if you purchased the book somewhere else. If you ever purchased anything on Amazon, you have an account. Your review need not be long. A fair, objective and authentic review is requested so others may benefit from your opinion. It need not be long, just a couple of well chosen sentences can be enough to help potential readers decide if the book is worth their time. Your opinion is valuable to both the author and the publisher.
The author-publisher team put a lot of effort into editing the manuscript before publication, but no book is perfect. If you notice an error, you could help improve future editions by emailing us with page number and line so it can be corrected.
Finally, if you enjoyed the book, be sure to tell your friends about it, in person and on social media such as Facebook, Twitter, LinkedIn and others.

Gene D. Robinson
publisher@moonshinecovepublishing.com

CPSIA information can be obtained at www.ICGtesting.com
Printed in the USA
BVOW08s1340101213

338663BV00003B/9/P